LAYOUT OF ADVERTISING AND PRINTING

LAYOUT OF ADVERTISING AND PRINTING

THIRD EDITION

Layout

The Practical Application of the Principles of Design to Advertising and Printing

By Charles J. Felten

NEW YORK · APPLETON-CENTURY-CROFTS, INC.

741.67
F34c

AUG 11 '55

Photographs by LEW KELLIE
Lettering and sketches by the Author

Copyright, 1947, 1949, by Charles J. Felten

Foreword . . .

MANY PRINTERS, writers, artists, and others to whom the creation of advertising and printing offers an incentive, may aspire to master layout but perhaps consider it an art to be practiced only by the professional.

The question is often asked: "Must I be a gifted artist, skillful letterer, or expert typographer to be a successful layout man?"

The answer is, that to practice layout in its fullest sense, as in the rendering of top-flight visuals for presentation purposes, one must have an abundant natural artistic ability and be highly trained in all phases of design, lettering and typography. One must also develop the faculty to co-ordinate these talents and accomplishments successfully. Anyone, however, who is adept at simple lettering, has acquired a comprehensive knowledge of the mechanics of typography and has learned to apply the elements of design, can render practical composing room layouts.

Realizing that a large percentage of layout enthusiasts may not be naturally proficient in drawing but nevertheless are creative-minded, the author has attempted to present this discourse on layout in an elementary yet informative manner, so as to benefit every printing planner.

Those whose artistic or typographical ability is more fully developed will also find in these pages much helpful material to augment their knowledge and talents.

The theories expounded and the techniques and procedures described are the result of many years of study and experience, and are based on that indispensable and time-proven factor—practicability.

C. J. F.

ACKNOWLEDGMENT

To over six thousand purchasers of the previous editions who have made this revised and enlarged third edition possible . . . to the reviewers, professors, teachers, students and craftsmen who have tested its worth . . . to the staff at *Printing* magazine who have given editorial help and encouragement . . . to the many advertisers represented herein and their agencies who have furnished reproductive material, particularly the Eastern Corporation whose type specimen sheets enrich these pages . . . to all my friends and fellow craftsmen who have aided in the preparation and printing of this volume . . . to all of them and to my good wife and family I dedicate this third edition.

C. J. F.

Contents

PART ONE

    PURPOSE · FUNCTIONS OF LAYOUT 1

    SCOPE OF LAYOUT 3

    LAYOUT STYLES 19

    LAYOUT SHAPES 23

PART TWO

    WORKING MATERIALS · TECHNIQUES 27

    FUNDAMENTALS OF LETTERING 37

    THUMBNAILS · ROUGHS · VISUALS 50

PART THREE

    ANALYZING THE COPY 56

    CHOOSING THE LAYOUT STYLE 59

    EVALUATING DISPLAY IMPORTANCE 63

PART FOUR

    BASIC DESIGN REQUISITES 67

        PROPORTION 67

        BALANCE 71

        CONTRAST 73

        RHYTHM 77

        UNITY 79

    FACING PAGE LAYOUTS 88

CONTENTS . . . *continued*

PART FIVE

    ALLOTMENT OF WHITE SPACE 91

    POSITIONING THE TRADE-MARK 96

    ORNAMENTATION 101

    REVERSE BACKGROUNDS · TONED AREAS . . . 104

PART SIX

    PHOTOGRAPHY · RETOUCHING · ART WORK . . 109

    CROPPING AND POSITIONING PHOTOGRAPHS . . 113

    PICTORIAL PERSPECTIVES 119

    APPLYING HAND LETTERING
        INITIAL LETTERS 122

    REPRODUCTION PROOFS · PHOTOPRINTS
        PHOTOSTATS 126

    PHOTOENGRAVING
        OTHER REPRODUCTIVE PROCESSES 128

PART SEVEN

    A SHORT STUDY OF TYPES 133

    FITTING COPY TO TEXT AREAS 149

    ACHIEVING EFFECTS WITH TYPOGRAPHIC
        MATERIAL 151

PART EIGHT

    COLOR—ITS EFFECTIVE APPLICATION 154

    SELECTING PAPER STOCK 163

    MARKING THE LAYOUT AND COPY 166

    PRACTICABILITY AND FLEXIBILITY 168

    THE QUICK BROWN FOX 170

LAYOUT OF ADVERTISING AND PRINTING

Purpose, Functions
of Layout

THE HUMAN EYE is the main physical avenue through which we comprehend all objects. Through this avenue impressions, reactions and desires are created in the mind.

To create favorable reactions, printing must be attractive in design; it should arrest the eye, hold the attention, impress and stimulate the reader, thereby fulfilling its fundamental purpose.

Everyone has an innate esthetic sense and appreciation of good design. The success that well-designed advertisements and printing achieve in stimulating interest is obvious.

Layout is the method of applying design to printing. It is the arrangement of all component parts, such as headlines, subheadings, text masses, illustrations, and signature into a unified, attractive pattern.

It is the accepted method in modern salesmanship and production of worthwhile advertising and printing. Through a comprehensive layout, ideas and copy become concrete plans for presentation, discussion, cost estimating and production procedures.

Layout is used in printing production as is an architect's blueprint in the construction of a building. As the erection of a beautiful home or any worthwhile structure stems from a well-planned combination of the artistic and utilitarian, so the effectiveness of printing and advertising depends upon the soundness of design and practicability of the layout.

Since printing and advertising are not stock-shelf commodities they must be custom-built to meet the needs of the product or service in which the reader is to be interested.

Every piece of copy has a theme or presents an idea around which an experienced layout man patterns an attractive design. No composition is too insignificant or unimportant to benefit from proper planning.

There was little need for layout in pre-historical times when the only method of visual communication consisted of chiseling figures in stone or inscribing characters on papyrus. With the invention of printing from movable type by Gutenberg in 1440, however, came the means and inspiration for artistic expression with ink and paper. The evolution of layout as an art stems from this era and has developed progressively with each advancement in typographic design.

The development of modern type-casting machines and high-speed precision presses has brought wide opportunities to the printing designer. It has made possible vast production of quality publication, direct-by-mail advertising and commercial printing. The need for top-flight designing and for efficient planning of mechanical procedures by means of accurate, detailed layouts is obvious.

Layout and design have kept step with modern mechanical developments. The current trend is toward simplicity of treatment and streamlined techniques. There is no time now for the leisurely hand-setting of frivolous ornamentation, or for the use of outmoded styles and techniques. Finer paper surfaces, highly-developed typographical equipment, improved photoengraving, offset and gravure techniques have given the printing planner modern tools and processes of inestimable value. Layout techniques are constantly being elaborated and the opportunities for their application are becoming more widespread.

All successful layouts must be built on sound structural lines and embody the fundamental layout requisites. Styles in typography and artistic techniques may change from year to year, but the fundamentals of good design remain the same.

Printing and advertising successfully compete for attention only when correct design is utilized in their production. Thus, every piece of printed matter can lift itself from mediocrity and accomplish its primary purpose —to be seen and read.

Scope of Layout

THE MECHANICS OF LAYOUT are adaptable to all branches of advertising and printing. The basic principles of design and the underlying procedures are as applicable to a business card as to a full-page advertisement. Practicability demands, however, that an appropriate design technique be applied to each individual format.

As a knowledge of many widely divergent types of layout is essential, we shall review briefly the scope of advertising and printing design.

Newspaper Advertising

Under this classification come the many types of advertisements appearing in daily and weekly newspapers. Here an advertisement competes for attention with a wide assortment of other ads, a large amount of reading matter, pictorial elements, a variety of headlines, subheads, boxheadings and other unrelated typography.

Considering fast production schedules and the constant remaking of daily newspaper pages for various editions, it is obvious that this type of layout presents more visual problems than does the planning of individually printed advertising matter.

Mindful of the cost of advertising space and the comparatively short time in which the reader must be attracted, it becomes apparent that top-notch newspaper layout is both an economic necessity and the most graphic means of imparting attention value to copy.

The outstanding qualities that effective newspaper layout should possess are attractiveness, individuality, appropriateness, and effective design and typographical contrast with surrounding advertising and text matter.

Mechanical limitations impose many restrictions on the layout of newspaper advertising, but the ad which combines the above qualities and effectively utilizes the fundamental design requisites in its construction has a better chance to be seen and read than a haphazard setting of so much type to fit a given space.

3

Full-page newspaper advertisements which have been made effective by sound planning, forceful layout and pictorial interest.

Below—Full-page magazine ads which utilize the utmost in layout, art techniques, typography and pictorial reproduction. Note the left- and right-hand page interest-directing elements in ads on both sides of the center ad.

Advertisement set by an "ad-agency typographer" for simultaneous reproduction in a full-sized paper and a tabloid.

Below—Attention-compelling pictures, interestingly cropped and forcefully displayed, give smaller magazine ads "reader interest."

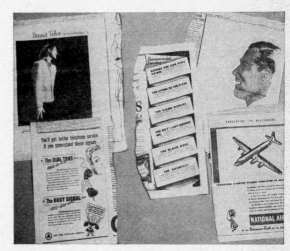

Attention-compelling display elements predominate in these two-, three- and four-column newspaper ads. Excellent examples of how interest may be directed by shapes and directional movement in pictorial elements. The girl at the left typifies an outside left-hand page position. The man's head and airplane ads are typical outside right-hand page ads.

The size of an advertisement is no criterion of its effectiveness. Many small advertisements have more attention value than their larger neighbors because the space has been better utilized by careful planning. Advertisements combining big, heavy type and blatant display elements, prevalent in much commonplace newspaper advertising, are often less effective than characterful advertisements that utilize conservative types and distinctively toned display units and masses that are properly displayed and accentuated. Interesting white space also, by contrast to an overcrowded composition, emphasizes a message which it surrounds and distinctly sets off.

Attention-compelling photographs and illustrations, with effective tone values, properly placed and skillfully cropped, add much to the effectiveness of newspaper advertising. Obviously, if the layout man can divert the attention of the reader from the news columns to the sales argument of a good picture advertisement, he gives that ad an initial advantage.

Department stores and other consistent users of newspaper advertising space seek to individualize their ads by adopting ingenious shapes of areas, novel treatments of name logotypes, trade-marks, borders and backgrounds, distinctive lettering and art techniques, and individualized typography.

Many advertisers have their newspaper layouts interpreted typographically by "ad agency shops"—typographers who specialize in the setting of advertisements to rigid standards of craftsmanship and refinement. These settings are then electrotyped, stereotyped or photoengraved in sufficient multiples to insure similar reproduction in all newspapers which print the advertisement. Thus a tabloid may print an ad, identical in all details, with one in a full-sized paper.

The average modern daily newspaper composing room, however, has a fairly comprehensive assortment of advertising display type, which offers the trained layout man wide opportunity to secure maximum results from advertising space.

Weekly newspaper advertising, which in the past was generally limited in style and attractiveness because it was usually produced with a minimum of layout and more restricted typographic facilities, is constantly being improved. Progressive weekly newspaper printers are continually adding

5

*In winning
a new market*

**DEPTH OF
PENETRATION**

is most important

Advertisers in THE CHRISTIAN SCIENCE MONITOR are constantly proving that this advertising sells goods and services. In this great international daily newspaper, their sales message penetrates right to the buying impulse of its readers.

Important, too, is the fact that MONITOR readers have far better than average buying power, especially for the worthwhile things in life. And leading retailers tell us that MONITOR readers make a point of asking for MONITOR-advertised products.

A planned program of MONITOR advertising will be a valuable stimulus to your business. May we draw up a detailed proposal custom-made for your product?—THE CHRISTIAN SCIENCE MONITOR, One, Norway Street, Boston 15, Massachusetts.

*News, Advertising, Readership
Devoted to Building a
Better Civilization*

SPEAKING OF DEPTH OF PENETRATION, HERE IS WHAT ONE ADVERTISER SAYS:
"We have tried a number of periodicals and other advertising methods, but we have come to the conclusion that the best returns come from your publication."

The CHRISTIAN SCIENCE MONITOR
An International Daily Newspaper

Branch Offices
NEW YORK: 500 Fifth Avenue
CHICAGO: 155 N. Michigan Avenue
DETROIT: 3-101 General Motors Building
KANSAS CITY: 1002 Walnut Street
SAN FRANCISCO: 624 Market Street
LOS ANGELES: 650 S. Grand Avenue
SEATTLE: 824 Skinner Building
PARIS: 16 Faubourg Saint Honoré
LONDON, W.C. 2: Connaught House, 163/4 Strand
GENEVA: 28 Rue de Cendrier

Listen every Tuesday night to
"THE CHRISTIAN SCIENCE MONITOR VIEWS THE NEWS"
with Erwin D. Canham, Editor, over the ABC network

Forceful action graphically pictorializes the intangible expressed in the heading, in this newspaper ad. Note proper directional emphasis in illustration, to beginning of text.

if you trade with

Siam...

—*let your business profit from the Irving Trust's
specialized knowledge of this FAR EAST market*

IN PRE-WAR SIAM, Americans were a rarity. Today, Siam's need for goods which America alone can supply . . Siam's abundance of resources in world-wide demand . . . have attracted the attention of scores of American businessmen.

The Irving Trust Company offers to importers and exporters its intimate knowledge of this increasingly important market. Here, as well as throughout the Far East, we have long-established contacts. Our officers experienced in foreign trade make personal visits to these markets. Such first-hand, up-to-date information may be of considerable value to you.

You are invited to discuss Siamese or other foreign business with our Foreign Division officers without obligation.

IRVING TRUST
Company

ONE WALL STREET · NEW YORK 15, N.Y.

MEMBER FEDERAL DEPOSIT INSURANCE CORPORATION

Pictorial atmosphere combines with symbolical lettering to create a "far east" feeling in this newspaper ad, whose purpose is mainly institutional.

Your printed selling serves as a **BRIDGE** *to
help your sales staff reach your customers. But
your selling messages — combining striking
art, arresting copy and fine printing — need
a firm foundation — the paper you select to
assure an outstanding first impression. That
is why wise buyers of printing add the finishing touch of quality by specifying Oxford
Papers for their sales-in-print.*

DISTRIBUTORS IN 48 KEY CITIES,
COAST TO COAST **OXFORD PAPERS**
230 Park Ave., New York 17, N.Y.

*ATTENTION to printed selling is gained by a
striking combination of art, message and fine printing
—but the first impression is made by the paper you
choose to carry your selling message. Wise buyers of
printing rely on the finishing touch of Oxford Papers
. . . in any one of many fine grades . . . to command
attention for their sales-in-print.*

OXFORD PAPERS
230 Park Ave., New York 17, N.Y.
DISTRIBUTORS IN 48 KEY CITIES, COAST TO COAST

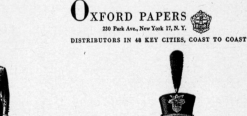

Two of a series of distinctive trade magazine advertisements which help to create good will and acceptance of the Company's product. Good perspective and rhythm effectively activate both patterns.

modern typographic equipment which makes possible a wider application of layout techniques.

Regardless of mechanical limitations, all newspaper advertising reflects the amount of planning used at its inception. That which is fundamentally sound in design will always be attractive, effective and successful.

Magazine Advertising

The vast assortment of advertising in popular magazines, periodicals, trade journals, house organs and other publications is included in this category.

Advertising competes for attention under more favorable conditions in a magazine than in a newspaper. Here more flexible production schedules and a wider variety of printing methods permit more colorful and elaborate presentations. Finer paper surfaces, likewise, enable a wider application of layout techniques and more latitude in art work, reflected in the use of finer screen tints, more elaborate reverse and combination plate treatments, and more detailed halftone presentations. As in newspaper layout, the same basic qualities of attractiveness, suitability, distinctiveness and contrast should predominate in every effective magazine advertisement.

In the quality magazines, artistic layout and modern craftsmanship in the graphic arts receive their fullest interpretation and here the national advertiser uses the ad-agency typographer even more extensively than in newspaper work.

The purchaser of costly advertising space has long since recognized the importance good layout plays in the presentation of his message. He regards it as a sound investment to use only the best photography, retouching, lettering and art work, fine typography, and highest quality photo-engravings.

Through the medium of fine color photography, color-process plates and highly developed multi-color printing, the layout man has a practically unlimited sphere for graphic presentation and originality. Full-color inserts, double-page spreads and other ingenious devices have enlarged the

At left is one of a series of "step-down" newspaper ads as it appeared in the *New York Times,* together with news matter to complete the page makeup. Below it is a reproduction proof of the ad alone showing the mortised section at top left for insertion of up-to-the-minute news matter by the publication.

Below is a silhouette halftone reduction made direct from a wash drawing by Dorothy Hood, one of America's outstanding fashion artists, who illustrated the series.

Below is a line reproduction made from a proof of another ad in the series also reduced from full-page size. The technique includes the setting of type to simulate the news columns in which the ads are to appear, cementing reproduction proofs of same to form a background pattern, cutting away a white area to silhouette the wash drawing, pasting display lines therein and casually hand lettering the Lord and Taylor logotype. Reproduced through kind cooperation of Lord and Taylor.

the Lord & Taylor Look

it is a

gold-brown-with-lace

theatre suit from

Don Loper's collection

(all ours alone)

365 00, on the Third Floor

We costume this suit with

beaded velours cap,

bronze bugle bead bag,

Newton Elkin's bronze slippers,

pale champagne gloves.

All from our

autumn collections.

LORD & TAYLOR'S COLLECTIONS REACH PEAK EXCITEMENT

For the next few weeks you will be seeing in these pages some of the highlights of our autumn and winter collections. You will find yourself studying them carefully — for silhouette, for detail — to see what little hat, what gloves, what bag, what shoes. (Will you be able to wear the exquisite brooch your grandmother has given you — it demands a dress of the most elegant stature, rich-textured — can you find it?)

For now, the age of elegance is here to stay. This means that assembling the dresses and suits and coats and accessories for the seasons ahead will afford you new pleasures — will give rein to feminity and imagination — may actually propel you into a new kind of life.

It means, moreover, that planning is essential. Every beautiful effect that will be achieved this season will stem from a dress or a suit or a coat that is an individual — calling for a very definite little hat, for one shoe and no other, for certain gloves, certain jewels. To put together more than one such costume, within your own financial limits, you must be clever about color — knowing about line and proportion — inspired about extras.

Planning Will Be a Ple

You will not begrudge the time you spend planning, the care you give to choosing the elements. For textures, colors, are all so very both mind and eye. But them now — as you study highlights from our collections — think how you can look for the new, exciting, elegant. Come in and see the new gloves, and note the way furs have an old-fashioned effect that adds with can be combined with handbags are not very small, but they become eerie, quite tiny for furs, handbags and evening. You will note the whole effect colors, a most subtle to both that will give a combine what you want different elements.

Brigance Fall & Winter Collection

Brigance's most extensive collection to date consists of suits and coats for both town and country, and a group of blouses and skirts coordinated in color and fabric to be worn interchangeably with the suits and coats. Wool town coats in rich deep tones are luxuriously lined with gleaming taffetas and bright silks. Blouses and skirts mirror the coats in color and fabric. A tweed country coat in a green plaid design shows a matching tweed skirt. A deep green wool town coat lined in striped green and black taffeta combines perfectly with a blouse and skirt in the same taffeta.

Blouses and skirts can also be intercombined. A taupe colored velveteen skirt is shown with three blouses in the same color but of different textures — velveteen, silk and linen. A black velvet short sleeved blouse frames the throat in an elongated "hoop neckline" and can be worn with a long stitched and pleated iridescent taffeta skirt or with a floor length snuff colored gabardine skirt.

Coats show fitted backs with the fullness concentrated at the center back between the shoulder blades and from there falling free. Other coats have long moulded torsos with the fullness released from the low dipping waistline. Sleeves are cut like a man's top coat in width so that coats slip easily over suits and leave the under sleeve smooth.

Suits have an elongated look with smooth fitted hips. Jackets are from twenty-four to twenty-six inches in length. A lush colored tangerine corduroy suit is a brilliant note for the cocktail or dining out scene. Another grey flannel suit is outlined in fine grey cord and accented with flat alabaster buttons.

Details — there is no hip padding. Fullness is either moderately gathered or pleated, never very full. Pockets slip into unpressed pleats. Hemlines are eleven inches from the floor. Vents held to linings shape the silhouette. Yokes turn into collars. Double breasted necklines descend into single breasted closings. Suit revers are square notched. Shadow lace stoles add a softening touch over blouses for

evenings. Throughout the collection, Brigance stresses rich textures in unusual combinations. An oxford grey coat concisely edged in black ribbed corduroy; a lace stole shadowing gabardine; velveteen with linen; crisp taffeta lining a wool coat.

Little Jewels Will Have Tremendous Importance

The important small jewel is one of those elements of fashion in which you can pin absolute faith. The little pieces — the minute, exquisite pins and clips — the delicate bracelets — the tiny drop earrings — the chokers of small pearls — these are the pieces of jewelry that look best with everything, simply everything. So we say — have beautiful earrings, have beautiful pins, have one beautiful bracelet. For you will wear them — or some one of them — with suits, late-afternoon dresses, soft wool — over and over and over.

You will find less interest ciful design — more interest and texture. Out of the the first new silhouette a flowing movement that are slim drawn — as if into a flare

You will find the new soft that total

Hands Look Soft and Small in New Gloves

We see a revival of interest in gloves with glace finish, many of them so seen on Paris where For the skin, and buttoned

The will be the mo taupe, a brown anything way of Look so set on black buttons with of the bodice.

Most sell ball are the f

Oleg Cassini has had an extensive background in the couture business. His career as a designer began in Italy in the early 1930's and continued to Paris where he sketched for some of the leading couturiers. He later came to this country and worked in New York's Seventh He finally emigrated

signing, Mr. Cassini is now permanently established in New York where he plans to design and produce

Firs Benenson Collection at Lord & Taylor Alone

Fira Benenson has set out to prove that the custom dressmaking tradition, with all its exacting refinements, can be successfully and practically transferred into the wholesale market. She feels that our national taste and way of life have developed to the point where the dress of subtle line, superior fabric and individual hand detail should be available to a larger public beyond the area of the custom salon. More and more women want clothes with a "made-to-order" feeling. With this in mind, Miss Benenson is showing a line indistinguishable from her couture collections, except that it is made in sizes.

The first Fira Benenson ready-to-wear collection is simple in an intricate way — a characteristic of this designer which has long baffled the people who try to describe it. By mosaic cutting, sometimes with as many as fourteen small sections to shape a waistline or eight separate parts joined to give a sleeve a special flare, the dress is moulded into flexible but definite outline. The decoration, too, is fused into the garment rather than added; dresses of crepe, satin or wool jersey have shirred inserts set in bands, curves, bowknots or others; sheer marquisette bands a broadcloth dress, to be figures

All American Designers Stress Silhouette

All Trigère's suits show medium long jackets with slightly flaring backs achieved by pleats, back peplums, and shirring set into a V at the small of the back. Skirts are not exaggeratedly full, but carefully worked to give smooth hang and ample width toward the hemline. Dresses have fitted sleeves, generally long and set into a natural shoulder, and show much back interest, frequently with descending fan shaped pleats at center back or again with shirring set into a low V or U line. Necklines are simple circular ones, fastening at the base of the throat like a string of beads — many high mounting turtle necks and up-winging collars.

Nettie Rosenstein's beautiful little black dresses and suits have both short jackets and longer peplum knits. She moves into a more romantic mood in her cocktail and evening story. Throughout is the feeling of two silhouettes — the straight and moulded and the flaring — where in the ankle-length, after-five dress one begins to hear the sophisticated rustle of which glasses are almost lower the shoulder itself seemingly slight at worm skirts when slit either obviously ats. Evening th, come in the figure rge but rsi w

Color News in Shoes

Below the dark ripple of taffeta, velvet, satin skirts — look for a glow of soft color in the slipper. If you wear black exceedingly well, you can do nothing more charming than to add emerald green or rosy red evening slippers to an otherwise all-black costume for dancing. But for less formal wear, we like the subtle tones — with a beige faille dress, a taupe velvet shoe, or olive green, or brown. For a brown wool costume, you must have velveteen shoes of a deep burnt tangerine. We have these, ready to wear.

Stockings Shadow Your Costume

The fad for dyed legs is out. Brigance, our own designer, sees stockings as a shadow of your costume — at once hinting of flesh tones and of the shade of dress or coat or shoe. Thus a taupe covert coat (Brigance has done a beautiful fitted one with tangerine shantung lining) would be completed with Shadow #4 — deep taupe overtones on a warm flesh tint. These Brigance-color stockings are ours alone, in five Shadow colors. Deepest — Shadow #5 — has been chosen to be worn with his costume of dark grey covert and black corduroy. The sheer nylon seems to flicker with black and grey shadows, reflecting first one and then the other texture.

Handbags Tell Time of Day

The separation between handbag for "life" and for afternoon is sharp, complete. Elegance is here to stay. The American woman has not altered the incredible activity of the day — her business engagements, her conferences with banker, with lawyer — her hospital committee meeting, her consultations with decorator.

For all the notes and statements and scraps of fabric and samples of color that are a part of this schedule, the daytime handbag hews close to the lines of the pouch. What we like above all is the new bag in soft leather, that begins in a small pouch or satchel or drawstring shape but is squashy extremely pliable.

As the afternoon grows, the becomes smaller and We like especially, the black suede bag with narrow handle, and clasp. Velvets and w and interesting, black satin bags small gold links. will look important narrow tweed about many of a fulled into a pleats.

Collection

horn brown ripline jacket d horn. The th shallow

grey fine lared prin ias folds of outline of irt. ress of slen fect outlined shirring with d in) at one pe day dress full skirt has a ar with big red the front. dress of mat black with ample, deeply bodice; jet buttons nt, full skirt with a attaching a deep bias e hemline. An afternoon black chiffon broadcloth is th narrow horizontal bands k marquisette with scattered not effects in each band. In a deep square neckline, mosaic at shaping the short sleeves into moderate puffs.

There is a classic dinner dress of pleated white-gold lame, the bodice diagonally pleated, the skirt full and flowing

The Little Hat Stays On

We take credit, here, for having turned the head of fashion in this direction fully a year ago. We said then — what with skirts getting wider and wider, and shoulders getting narrower and narrower — hats are bound to get smaller and smaller. They did. Now that the silhouette has crystallized into sloping shoulder, small waist, and sweeping skirt — look for more and more fascinating variations on the little hat.

You will see toques, pillboxes, cloches, tiny berets, all high in favor again. The fur pillbox is perfect above a flowing coat, has surprise value with a severely tailored suit. A beret looks good worn straight on the brow, with thin flowing silhouette — looks extremely new worn far to one side above the neat, nipped-in cardigan.

Hats like little caps take many shapes. Some are espoused flat, and tie under the chin. Others are mushroomed, with buttons on top. Still others shape to the head, with small visors. Look for the texture to add interest — rabbit's-hair skimmers, plushly velvets and velours, velveteen, jersey

The little hat of autumn 1948 is the most beautifully trimmed of any hat in years. Never anything startling — anything shooting out at a tangent. But exquisite edging, braids, little tassels and soutache, shapely feathers, a length of rich-hued ribbon. By their detail they add immeasurably to the elegance of your costume.

Think Briefly of Your Hair

We would not add anything to this detail of your ensemble — we would subtract. Keep your hair short, keep your hair close, keep it turned up in a gentle curve on the cheek.

Do this one small thing for the sake of your hat, your little coat, your new little furs — the great thing will be what they do for you.

field of design possibilities in magazines immensely. The attractive color pages of the smarter magazines offer much inspiration for the study of contemporary styles and techniques in layout. The progressive layout man will find it advantageous to collect outstanding examples of magazine advertising containing unique art, lettering, photoengraving and typographical techniques, for reference and inspiration.

Editorial Layout

The creation of the "editorial" type of layout—that which embodies the design of the pages of a publication or periodical in which text and pictures are combined—differs greatly from the usual "product selling" layout.

The basic purpose of an "editorial" type layout is to create interest by attractive presentations of pictorial elements, typographical arrangements and decoration, to enhance the editorial content of the publication and make it inviting to read. A style of treatment that befits the class of readers, their tastes, habits and customs, likewise is an objective.

There are many types of publications—popular, class, trade and others. Their individualized appeals, their editorial objectives and their relative styles of make-up differ greatly.

Assuming that the general treatment or over-all style pattern for art, photographs and typographical techniques has been established, the procedure for layout generally follows this course:

Each story in manuscript form is carefully read to establish an illustrative theme. Penciled notations are made as to tempo, period, locale, physical characteristics of characters, and many other details. Some text may offer spontaneous clues for outstanding illustration, while other copy may prompt predominating typographical arrangements with subordinated illustrations.

As each story or article crystallizes, small thumbnail sketches are made for evaluating ideas. From them roughs are made on previously printed layout tissues which portray regulation page dimensions.

These roughs make preliminary evaluation of the size, shape, tone and position of all illustrative and typographic elements, but are not final or absolute. They remain variable and flexible until the pagination of the entire "book" is evaluated as a unit. It is obvious that a page layout that may appear well designed in itself may need readjustment and refinement when placed opposite another. Although spreads of the same story may remain as originally designed units, the single opening or closing pages of a story may need modification or elaboration according to the pagination.

Ofttimes the need of a definite color in the illustrations may require the shifting of entire spreads or individual opening or closing pages to fit the mechanics of pressroom production. Editorial rearrangement of pages may necessitate subtle changes in layout pattern to make pages more harmonious (or contrasting) without deviating materially from the original conception.

Styles and placements of headings and their relationships to the pictorial elements are practically limitless. It is logical, at one time, to employ an all-capital one-line heading in a formally balanced arrangement and change to a lower case roman or italic in an informal arrangement on the next page to maintain that change of pace or variety that instills interest.

Layout of magazine text pages involves an endless variety of procedures and requires individualized treatment to suit specific requirements. Adaptations of the basic design principles treated in subsequent pages are applicable to magazine text page layouts; likewise to the many diversified layout problems encountered in trade papers, house organs and other publications.

Direct Mail Advertising

To receive favorable attention today, direct mail advertising material, which includes folders, booklets, pamphlets, broadsides, blotters, and other mailing pieces, must be more attractive than ever before. With the vast amount of matter being sent through the mails, and the competition a mailing piece meets on the prospect's desk, it is essential that its physical appearance arouse enough interest to insure its perusal by the recipient.

In the design of direct mail advertising the layout man has increased opportunities in the many sizes, colors, weights and finishes of paper stock. He likewise has the advantage of a practically unlimited choice of format, more controllable methods of reproduction and wider latitude in typesetting, photoengraving, presswork and bindery procedures.

That the design of direct mail advertising should reflect the individuality and character of the product or service it represents is obvious. Likewise, every structural element, such as size, shape, and color should accentuate the design.

The evolution of a mailing piece that is unhampered by the restrictions of conventional commercial envelope sizes allows great freedom. This does not suggest that stock paper sizes and press restrictions should be ignored. They are practical factors in the economical production of all printing.

*Right—*A variety of editorial type layouts interpreted in printed form. All specimens were in two colors and show application of contrast in size, shape, tone and position between headline and pictorial elements, which creates interest in the text of the publication.

An editorial page rough for one of the printed pages shown at the right.

The design of direct mail printing utilizes the most individualized type of layout and reproductive processes.

Magazine editorial layouts that have graphic expressiveness in pictures, headlines, subheads and text, create attention and readability.

In designing a book, its functional purpose should be emphasized throughout the treatment of cover, title and text pages.

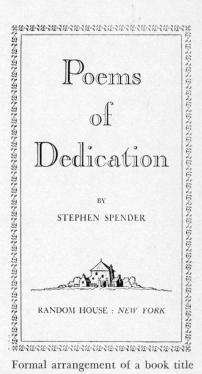

Poems
of
Dedication

BY

STEPHEN SPENDER

RANDOM HOUSE : NEW YORK

Formal arrangement of a book title page, designed by Meyer Wagman.

While most direct mail advertising is designed to produce immediate results, the institutional type may be planned to develop and maintain good will over a period of time. Success in this form of advertising is achieved by continuity in design and constant repetition of some pleasing general theme or identifying format.

Successful direct mail advertising stems from a careful analysis of purpose, searching study of the copy mood, correct choice of format, layout style and treatment, proper choice of stock, fine typography, good art work, the best obtainable photography and proper reproduction procedures.

Container Design; Display Advertising

This classification embraces labels, packages, containers, display cards and posters, the design of which demands a faster tempo and more dynamic appeal than that which is read more leisurely.

The success of a label or container depends on the instant "eye appeal" it has, in a window, on a counter or shelf. Likewise, a display card or poster must be so forceful and compelling as to impress the reader at first glance.

Much research is necessary in this highly specialized phase of design. When one considers the wide variety of cosmetics, foods and other products, preparations and commodities, it is obvious that the size, shape, color and design technique of both container and display advertising must promote a definite quality, characteristic of other sales appeal under widely varying conditions and amid changing surroundings.

As fullest utilization should be made of all printing, gravure and lithographic processes in combination with die cutting and other specialized finishing processes, the designing of containers and display advertising should be done only with the cooperation of reproduction experts whose technical advice and recommendations should be highly regarded.

Commercial Printing

Under this classification come letterheads, cards, envelopes, billheads, forms, hand bills, tickets, programs, and other miscellaneous items, commonly termed "job printing."

Most important is the letterhead. It is through this medium that the recipient usually receives his first impression of the sender. If it is poorly designed, shoddily printed on a cheap paper, sent in an unmatched envelope, the reaction is invariably unfavorable. On the other hand, a well planned, nicely balanced, tastefully composed letterhead, colorfully printed on a characterful paper stock, creates a favorable impression and imparts confidence.

In the layout of an effective letterhead, great care must be exercised to keep the general treatment characterful but not obtrusive. Uniqueness and smartness are desirable but restraint should be practiced in range of type sizes, tonal values and utilization of space. Most effective results can be obtained by skillfully accentuating name, product or trade-mark, in relation to other minor type blocks, while maintaining harmonious balance and tone.

Letterhead design should never interfere with utility. Practicability dictates that ample room should always be allowed for the writing of the message. The address and phone number should be prominently displayed.

In many cases, the change from the usual letterhead to the smaller "Monarch" size adds dignity, particularly for lawyers, architects, or other professional clients.

Colored stock should be used only when it fits the character of firm or service. A pastel pink letterhead is fitting for a flower shop, but would not be appropriate for a dentist or a lawyer.

Once a design has been established for a letterhead, the accompanying envelope, billhead, and card should evolve from the same idea and embody the same general treatment in design, typography and color combination.

Tickets, posters, hand bills, programs and journals for dances or entertainments are generally produced at competitive prices, but there is no need to neglect design in their preparation. It is surprising what can be accomplished through the application of the basic layout requisites, intelligent use of color, and careful type choice in this kind of printing.

Attractive compositions, carefully planned on the drawing board, outweigh in attention value and appearance the ones set "right out of the case."

The headings in the two ads above use distinctively different methods of approach in copy, but both agree that one of the most effective ways of selling a product is by pictorializing it. These daily newspaper ads (both reduced about one half) utilize the basic design requisites, discussed at greater length in a later chapter, in a most successful manner. The John Ward ad is a formal, or symmetrically balanced pattern in which good *proportion*, subtle *balance*, definite *contrast* (emphatic display of the product), *rhythm* and *unity* are exemplified. The A & P ad is an outstanding specimen of a faster moving, rhythmic, informal composition which carries the eye swiftly through the pattern to assimilate all elements in a logical manner terminating at the logotype which definitely emphasizes the brand name.

The experimental pencil rough at left shows how movement may be introduced in a formal layout by means of an activated hand-lettered heading whose descending diagonal connects it with the product, text and the name logotype at bottom.

Ad reproductions are line cuts.

Left panel shows pencil rough for a folder and the printed piece. Note change in copy from original rough which did not affect the basic design pattern. An example of how effective layout can facilitate the mechanics of typesetting and printing in such simple form as adequately as in the more elaborate presentations.

Below are layouts wherein a basic design pattern is repeated, in varying adaptations, in letterhead, notehead, card, envelope, announcement and other printed pieces. Black and one color (illustration) are suggested in what is commonly termed "two-color" printing.

Fresh, modern booklet covers attract and invite reader interest. These examples combine the type styles mentioned with harmonizing patterns. Colorfully printed on serviceable stock, they are handy for reference when copy-fitting.

Paper manufacturers are keenly aware of the sales value of attractively designed presentations of their products, as illustrated below. A calligraphic rendering of a design symbol harmonizes with calligraphic lettering. Calligraphy is more fully described in a later chapter.

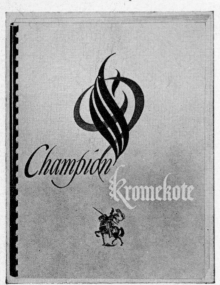

A simple tissue-paper layout, designating type sizes, text masses, borders, etc., will save much guessing and resetting in the composing room.

Designing business and office forms is primarily a matter of utility, but layout can play an effective part in intelligent planning of space, and adaptability to purpose. Much time can be saved in composition of rule forms and making of wax plates if the form is accurately ruled beforehand.

Book Design

The design and layout of books is most deeply rooted in tradition. The treatment of title pages, chapter headings, margins and other functional design elements has seen little material change in the many years since Gutenberg printed the first Bible. Few books have excelled those of the early bookmakers in basic design and beauty. Most contemporary book design is original mainly as to typographical usages and novel adaptations of materials and processes.

Application of sound modern layout techniques in certain types of books is refreshing and adds sparkle to the graphic presentation. The layout style, however, must be definitely suited to the theme and purpose of the book. A novel, which is mostly typographical, obviously demands different treatment than an educational book which is largely pictorial. The novel requires an attractive typographical treatment to interest the reader continuously through the entire story with only an occasional pause for change in literary pace. The book you are now reading was designed to direct particular interest to the pictures, which, by their straightforward story-telling technique, demand the unadorned simplicity of a modern layout that tells the story in a concise, forceful manner.

The scope of book design encompasses a practically unlimited array of novels, textbooks, reference books, manuals and other diversified books.

Choice of layout should be made only after careful consideration of the title and purpose of the book and the most practical interpretation of its copy, illustrations and other elements.

The lower left ad symbolizes the formal or symmetrically balanced layout style, while the top right ad is typical of the informal or asymmetrically balanced style. Both are outstanding examples of the proper utilization of white space for effective contrast.

Layout Styles

FUNDAMENTALLY, there are but two distinct layout styles—the *formal,* or symmetrically balanced, and the *informal,* or non-symmetrically balanced.

The former is based on the traditional design principle of controlling harmonious balance in a centered arrangement. The latter typifies the dynamic design principle of maintaining both movement and equilibrium in a non-centered arrangement.

Formal Layout

This style of layout is used primarily in compositions of a conservative, dignified and reposeful nature. It imparts a sense of restraint and stability.

The design basis for formal layout is the placing of all display elements such as pictures, display lines, text masses, signature cuts, etc., in an absolutely centrally balanced arrangement within the layout area.

To explain more fully, if a vertical line is drawn absolutely in the center of an area, every display element must be so centrally placed thereon, horizontally, as to be an equal distance from both left and right extremities; and each element that appears on one side of this vertical line must be duplicated in a corresponding position on the other side to maintain harmonious balance.

Design in a formal layout is achieved by correctly accentuating certain display elements, harmoniously contrasting their sizes, shapes and tones.

19

properly proportioning the widths of display lines, correct grouping and leading of headings and text masses, proper use of margins and white space, effective ornamentation and proper placing of the composition vertically within the layout area.

Formal layout usually predominates in financial, professional and institutional advertising; likewise in ecclesiastical, social and other formal printing where reserve and tradition are exemplified.

Informal Layout

This style of layout embraces the many varieties of off-centered arrangements that depend, to one degree or another, on the momentum of the design to attract attention, invite interest and activate the reader.

Informal layout was developed in comparatively recent years to meet the demands for newer design techniques and faster tempo in advertising and printing. It stems from the principle of creating movement in a design by placing all units and masses in a lively, orderly progression, and, by so doing, dividing a layout area into unusual and interesting patterns of tone and white space while maintaining an optical balance.

Adaptations of the informal layout style are practically limitless and may be applied to a composition in varying dynamic degrees, depending on the results to be accomplished.

The so-called "modern" layout is an extreme evolvement of informal layout which was developed from geometric design. Its chief characteristics are simplicity of line and movement. The combination of units and masses into interesting geometric arrangements, the division of white space into forceful contrasting elements and the elimination of fussy ornamentation are other distinguishing features of this style. It is further accentuated by the prolific use of sans-serif types, bleed illustrations, reverse panels, screen tint backgrounds and other contemporary design devices.

Formally-balanced layout   Informally-balanced layout

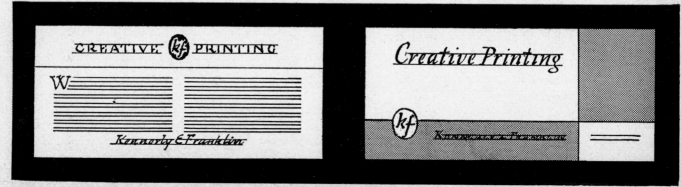

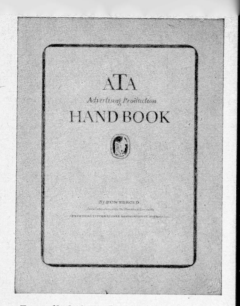

Formally-balanced title page layout in which contrast in size, shape and tone in the display lines is attained with a degree of restraint.

The thumbnail sketches in right panel and on the next page show a cross-section of the wide variety of patterns adaptable to newspaper, magazine direct mail and poster advertising.

Informal or asymmetrical layouts predominate in the showing as this type of layout is more generally used in modern-day advertising because it typifies a faster-moving tempo than does the formal or symmetrically-balanced style of layout.

The *formal* style is illustrated in the layouts titled "Charm" at upper right, "Formali" and "Distinction" at lower left. In these small crayon roughs the principle of balancing all display elements on a central vertical axis is exemplified. If an element is placed to left or right of this vertical, it must be counterbalanced by a unit of similar size and weight on the opposite side of the vertical. Limited movement may be attained by ingenious arrangements that create interest, but still maintain balance, as illustrated by the "Formali" layout.

Continued on next page

Continued from previous page

The various types of *informal* layouts stem basically from lively interesting space divisions and ingenious, contrasting patterns. Movement may be slow, fast, or of an intermediate tempo dependent upon the design pattern, the directional shapes of the elements and their arrangement. Slow movement in informal arrangements is exemplified in the layouts titled "'Flower Show," "Fishing" and "Pattern" at the upper right. Faster moving examples are the miniature roughs titled "Flavor," "Gracious Living" and "Parkay" at the upper left. In the "Interiors" and "Scenic Tours" sketches in the lower right, action is stimulated by the directional movement of the illustrations. Intermediate action is typified by layouts "Comfort," and "Men Who Care."

A layout which is fundamentally formal in arrangement, but by virtue of informal placement of one or two elements becomes informal in style, is illustrated by the "Integrity" layout at bottom left.

Informal arrangement for a newspaper ad which emphatically contrasts the heading in no uncertain tone.

Layout Shapes

Vertical or Horizontal Layouts?

The broad, expansive area of the horizontal layout tends to influence the designer's choice towards the dynamic informality of the asymmetrical type of layout for utmost effectiveness in proportioning and space divisioning. The vertical layout, on the other hand, seems to influence the choice of the more conventional, formal or symmetrically balanced style of layout. This is due primarily to the limited layout width which cannot be as readily divided without creating impractical narrow areas for headlines, pictorial and textual elements.

The choice of layout style need not be made arbitrarily, however, and certain characteristics of both formally and informally balanced styles may be combined effectively in the preliminary thumbnails.

The main objective is to divide every layout into non-mathematical areas or divisions of space and to place therein well-proportioned display and text elements that will attract and interest the eye and influence the readability of the message.

In horizontal layouts, the display lines may disport themselves in much wider areas than in the vertically shaped area where heads may have to be displayed in two or three lines to attain shape harmony with the narrower but deeper vertical area.

In horizontal layouts, over-wide text masses are avoided by breaking up a contemplated horizontal text element into two- or three-column elements in the same relative area. Thus vertical rhythm is introduced to offset the monotony of a static horizontal element.

In vertical layouts, on the other hand, very narrow text masses should be avoided. The general rule that type must not be set in too wide a measure for good readability has its counterpart in the principle that it likewise should not be set too narrow and cause undue letter and word spacing which affects its readability and tone value in mass.

The layout of a horizontal area generally requires more skillful proportioning of space and allocation of elements than does the vertical style.

Tendency to utilize repetitious horizontal elements only in such a broad area must first be overcome if utmost variety and interest are to be achieved, regardless of whether a formally balanced or informally balanced design is to be employed.

The symmetrical arrangement of a formally balanced layout may be desired in compositions of a reserved nature. But, so that the dynamic qualities of informal layout may also be fully evaluated, we limit our experiments in the former style and stress the latter in the accompanying sketches.

In the formal style, the equality of margins at the left and right sides is the uniformity that offsets the irregularity of the top and bottom margins, the proportionate widths of display lines, subheads, pictorial elements, signature and other elements.

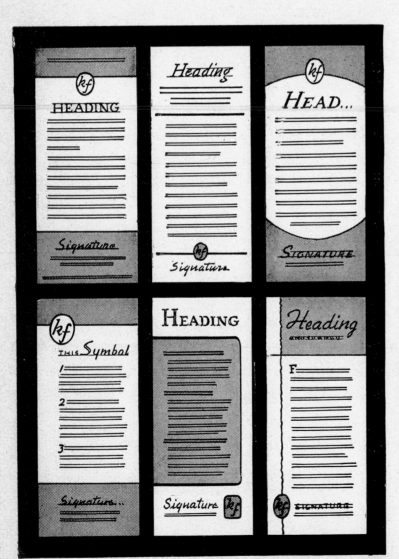

The vertical sketches at left stress the importance of building thumbnails with variations of size, shape, tone and position of the component elements based on the fundamental technique of dividing the layout area effectively.

Below—The left and top examples show vertical and horizontal shape harmony as described in the text. The three lower right thumbnail sketches show the basic space division of the vertical area into non-mathematical areas. This is more fully discussed in a later chapter.

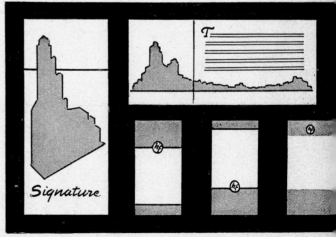

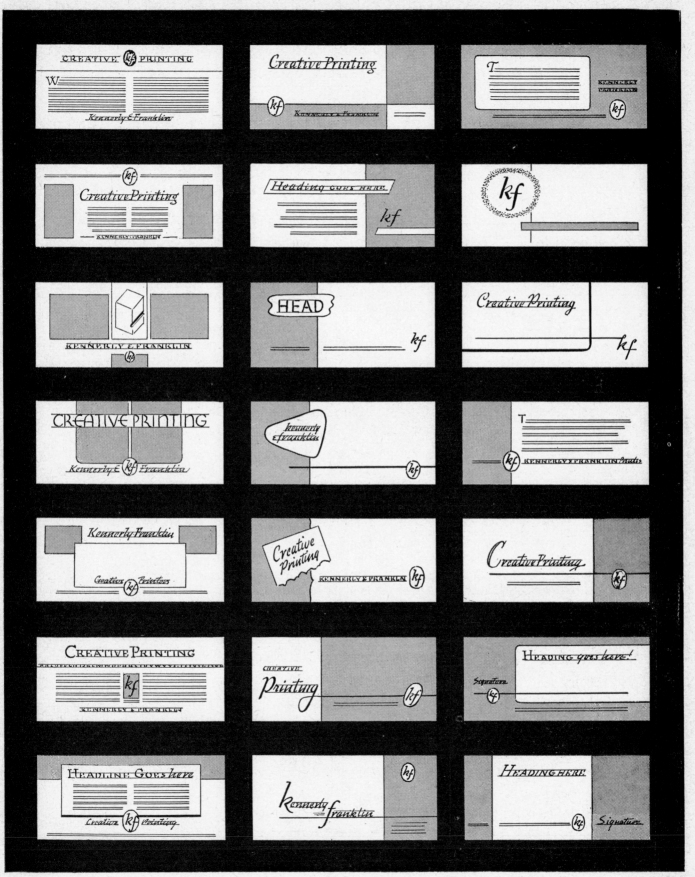

Wide, horizontal layout areas may be interestingly divided by the techniques shown above.

Obviously, the space divisioning must be done with due regard to the relative attention value, size, shape and tone of display elements and the space required for textual elements and other subordinate material.

Variety in shapes of areas and elements creates visual movement and interest. The eye reacts to things that are alive and rejects those that are static. However, variety should not be overdone.

Vertically shaped elements are said to influence visual movement downward or upward; horizontal elements to the left or right. This principle should be applied in the preliminary thumbnails and, if found applicable to all the layout elements in the enlarged, actual size tissue-paper rough, can forestall weak, indecisive patterns.

Generally, the shape of a predominating display element influences the choice of a horizontal or vertical layout for a blotter. For example, if the main illustrative element is a skyscraper, a vertical shape will accentuate its height and offer the designer opportunities to contrast pleasing horizontal elements in the design. On the other hand, an expansive skyline or horizon view would generally require a horizontal layout area.

In a creative process so widely variable as modern layout practice, the more experienced designer utilizes many ingenious patterns, procedures and techniques that depart from the conventional. Thus, he avoids the trite and commonplace.

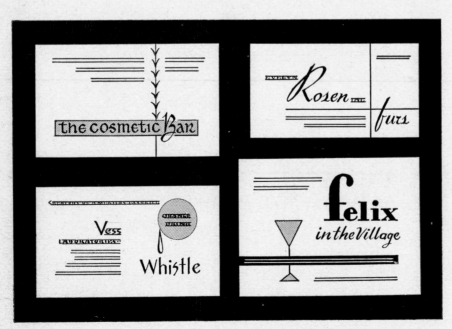

The four thumbnails at left show how variation in size and shape of a business card can be regulated to emphasize the theme and character of a business, service or product. Likewise, how the contrasting shapes of the textual, illustrative and decorative elements create emphatic visual movement that effectively activates each pattern.

While a business card is traditionally horizontal, it may often be enlarged vertically to increase the effectiveness of a design such as in the "felix" example.

Working Materials
Techniques

WHILE IT IS TRUE that layouts are evolved in the mind, the physical process of rendering them can be facilitated immeasurably with the aid of proper instruments and equipment. The layout man who is handicapped by poor tools is at a distinct disadvantage.

Not all of the items listed below are absolutely essential to the beginner, but real need will be found for all of them as advancement is made in the many diversified layout techniques.

The layout kit should contain:

Drawing board
T-square
Triangles
French curves
Metal-edge ruler and pica gauge
Protractor
Ruling pen and compass set
Pads of tracing paper
Thumb tacks
Cellulose and masking tape
Drawing pencils
Drawing pens
Water color brushes
Plastic eraser
Set of opaque water colors
Fixatif and atomizer

Color-mixing pans
Waterproof black India ink
Transparent colored inks
Colored pencils
Colored pastel sticks
Sandpaper pencil pad
Grease marking pencil
Razor blades
Type gauge
Reducing glass
Enlarging glass
Screen finder
Slide rule
Rubber cement and dispenser
Shears
Cropping angles

A wide assortment of paper of various textures, colors, and weights should always be kept on hand. Paper manufacturers have experimented extensively with color and design possibilities and their agents will furnish sample sheets and dummies for layout purposes on request.

Foundry type, linotype, monotype and Ludlow type specimen books should be collected until one has a comprehensive library of every type face in reasonable use.

If a layout man works closely with any one composing room, he should have proofs of all its type, set in a convenient measure of about five inches in width, for quick computation of display lines and text, and for tracing purposes. Proofs of ornaments, fancy initials and other accessories likewise will facilitate sketching same on layouts.

Specimen sheets showing the range of halftone screens and the variety of Ben Day shadings available in photoengraving and offset are invaluable for reference when planning tone values on layouts.

Printing ink color specimens, from which proper color tones can be evaluated and specified, should be included in the layout kit.

A "morgue" or clipping library is an inspirational source for ideas when layouts are hurriedly demanded. In it may be filed samples of interesting layout styles, type arrangements, color treatments, initial letters, unusual photoengraving and offset techniques and other interesting artistic specimens. It should contain, likewise, a wide assortment of pictorial reproductions rendered in various artistic mediums, which may often be adapted to layouts by tracing or copying, with necessary modifications or elaborations of structural form or surface style.

The successful layout man constantly profits by emulating the successful experiences of fellow craftsmen. By continuous study and use of time-tested formats, procedures and methods, he eventually acquires many invaluable ideas which will assist him in making a sound analysis of each layout problem as it arises.

Distinctiveness for a layout is many times achieved by coordinating its essential design elements according to the pattern of a previously successful composition. The helpfulness of a complete reference file is obvious.

Many layout men accumulate collections of "befores and afters" which contain the initial roughs, progressive working layouts, intermediate proof sheets and the finished printed jobs. They offer an excellent basis for study of idea development through both the artistic and mechanical phases.

Authoritative books on photography, lettering, art techniques, typography, color application, photoengraving, presswork, and other branches of the graphic arts should always be handy for ready reference. One should likewise subscribe to the leading technical periodicals of the printing and allied industries to keep abreast of constantly improving mechanical processes and techniques.

Suggestions for Layout Procedure

The layout beginner who constantly takes pains in perfecting apparently inconsequential details will find his layouts gradually attaining a professional look. This is not to say that they should be mechanically stilted, but they should embody a combination of artistic expressiveness and preciseness.

It is practically impossible to lay down rigid rules for the layout beginner to follow in the utilization of the various materials and equipment. In every creative endeavor there are limitless ways in which one may apply himself and each individual finds from experience alone in what manner he can work to best advantage. However, the following rudimentary suggestions may be helpful:

One should select a medium-sized non-warping drawing board and learn to adjust it to suit his own individual drawing posture. It should be placed in the lap, resting against a table or desk, at an angle that allows utmost freedom and dexterity.

As one progresses in layout, it will be found advantageous to use the more elaborate table-type drawing stand which can be adjusted to any desired angle.

The tracing pad or paper dummy should be fastened to the board in a high-centered position parallel to the top and sides of the board so that lines drawn with the T-square and triangle will be uniform to the edges of the paper. When ruling the dimensions of a layout area and other rectangular lines thereon, use the T-square placed along the left edge of the board for horizontal lines and the right angle triangle placed against the T-square for vertical lines.

When sharpening pencils, expose about a quarter inch of lead, and use the sandpaper pad to keep the required point for the style of lettering or rendering to be done. For drawing thin-serifed types and other delicate

Here are some tools of the layout man. Shown are various types of pencils, colored crayons, a plastic eraser, a French curve and other appurtenances.

The layout man must familiarize himself with the techniques of drawing and painting on various paper stocks in all mediums. Shown are pencil, crayon, pen and brush treatments.

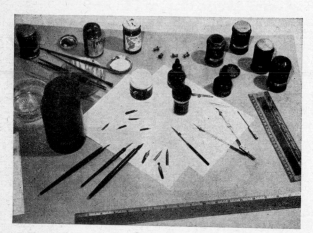

Among other necessary layout instruments are pica rule, compass, pens, slide rule, rubber cement, brushes, water colors and inks.

Placing a tracing tissue over type specimens and tracing them is good practice for the beginner.

Every layout man should keep abreast of typographical and reproduction trends by reading the leading technical publications of the graphic arts industry.

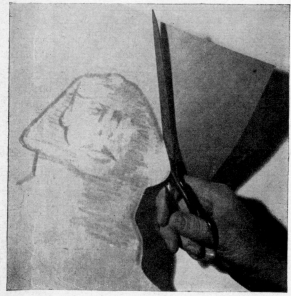

Irregularly shaped paste-ups can be trimmed best with the shears. A razor blade against a steel rule cuts rectangular shapes best.

lines one should use a fairly hard pencil with a sharp point. For drawing sans-serif or even-tone types and designating broader tones a softer pencil with a flat point should be used. Always use a hard pencil for denoting trim sizes of layouts and keep the lines comparatively faint.

One will become accustomed to favorite gradations of pencil lead, but it will be found that the B grade is the most practical for casual roughing of thumbnail sketches and for suggesting pictorial elements on layouts. Where broader, less detailed tones are desired the 2B, 4B or 6B grade is recommended.

Parallel horizontal lines are generally used for designating type lines in a text area. Their weight should suggest the approximate type tone, the space between these parallel lines suggesting the point size of the type. Type masses may also be drawn with strokes of a broad-pointed sketching pencil sharpened to the proper width.

Tracing paper offers an inviting surface for a drawing pencil and its gray tone enhances the artistic quality of a rough. Its transparency simplifies the application of color on its reverse side, which produces soft, pastel tones in the colored areas.

The advantages of working on transparent tracing tissue are many. If, for instance a layout is pretty well established, and proportions, sizes, shapes, groupings, spacing or margins are not satisfactory, a new tissue may be placed thereon and units reshaped, resized and shifted to improve the composition. Pictures, type, initial letters, trade-marks, or other elements which have been traced may be transferred to a dummy by rubbing the reverse of the tracing with a soft graphite pencil, placing it in positive position and going over the desired area on the front of the tissue with a well-pointed pencil. The tracing should be handled gently so as not to smudge the dummy. Excess graphite may be removed with the plastic eraser.

In the rendering of lettering or sketches on presentation visuals some layout men are highly proficient with the pen, while others prefer the brush. Use of the medium that best suits one's technique is logical.

Drawing pens are available in every conceivable style and one should have a good assortment, varying from the needle-pointed crow-quill for delicate work, to the broad-pointed speed-ball type for the uniform heavy strokes.

Brushes that have a pointed tip, Nos. 1 to 6, are best for inking and coloring on layouts. Show-card brushes of the rounded variety are good for simplified one-stroke lettering, for filling in areas, and other work of this nature.

Opaque show-card water colors are best for average layout work. One should avoid over-diluting colors to prevent the painted surface from becoming streaked, uneven in tone and messy in appearance.

Water color of the proper consistency can be applied successfully to most papers with the ruling pen or compass. Wherever possible these instruments should be used to get sharp, clean edges to the edges of broad color areas. Certain types of lettering on visuals may be constructed basically with the ruling pen but proficient free-hand finishing will give a more artistic appearance.

The rougher paper textures may, at first, tax the ingenuity of the layout student, but by constantly experimenting with pencil, crayon, pen and brush on various types of papers, he will solve these problems eventually.

Where large areas of color are to be shown on a layout and lettering or other elements are to be superimposed thereon, paper of the selected color can be cut to the size of the area, pasted in position and drawing done thereon more readily than by drawing over a painted surface. Lettering done directly on transparent cellulose may also be effectively placed over painted areas of a layout.

"Punch" can be added to a finished layout by adding well-placed strokes of a medium-soft dark-lead pencil to emphasize display lettering and other important elements. One should avoid the use of heavy pressure on the pencil, rather attaining depth of tone values by repetitious uniform strokes. Where water colors are to be applied over pencil lettering, use the pencil lightly as the graphite tends to darken the color and give a muddy effect. This applies also to drawing or lettering that is to be finished in ink or colored crayon.

Rubber cement is practically indispensable to the layout man. It is

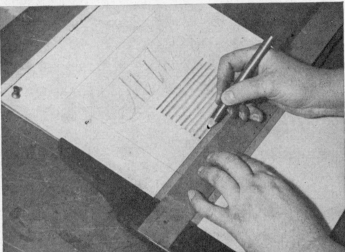

Left—The four illustrations show in consecutive order:

With the tracing pad held firmly in position with thumbtacks, the proper alignment of the T-square and right-angle triangle will insure a rectangular uniformity in dimensions.

Text masses are designated with parallel horizontal strokes of the correct width of pencil.

Puncturing the four corner points of the established type area through the entire dummy with compass point or pin facilitates ruling identical areas on all subsequent pages.

By placing a straight piece of paper over the irregular edge of a ruled text area and erasing the superfluous graphite, a clean, straight edge results.

The diagonal method of enlarging an area proportionately consists of extending the diagonal drawn from top left to bottom right of the picture, to either the height or width wanted and then drawing a parallel to the other dimension.

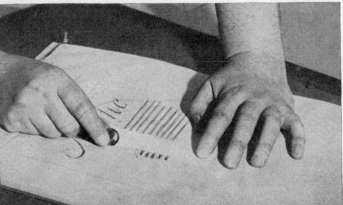

To draw an enlargement of a picture by the "square" method, rule rectangles on a tissue covering the entire picture (extreme left). Rule the same amount of squares on the enlarged area and use each square as a guide in sketching the elements within it.

used for pasting photostats, pictures, proofs and practically any porous material. Good quality cement is stainless and excess applications may be rubbed off with the finger when dry. For a temporary adhesion, one coating to either object suffices. The paste-up may later be lifted for change of position. For permanent adherence, apply cement to both objects and join when each has dried. Care must be exercised, however, to place them in exact position before bringing them together, as the two dry coatings have permanent affinity for one another and cannot be shifted.

Dividers are invaluable for checking alikeness of margins, spacing and other measurements on layouts, proofs and press sheets.

The plastic eraser is best for eradicating fingermarks and messiness caused by excessive pencilling and smudging. If minor mistakes occur in ink or color applications, light, dexterous touches of the razor blade can correct them, but care must be exercised lest the paper surface be ruined.

One should never use a razor blade against a triangle, T-square or other valuable instrument. Instead, use the metal edge of an inexpensive ruler for guidance when cutting or trimming paper, pictures or photostats. Keep the hands and fingers out of the range of the blade at all times. Shears should be used for cutting irregular shapes.

Use of a reducing glass aids in visualizing reduction possibilities and limitations in photographs, art work, lettering, and type proofs.

The enlarging glass is invaluable in checking type, halftone screens and color proofs, press sheets, and the numerous details of reproduction.

The transparent screen finder, which, when placed over printed halftone proofs, portrays their correct screens, is useful in checking the printability of cuts on a contemplated stock.

The slide rule is an invaluable instrument for quickly establishing dimensional ratios, such as in enlarging and reducing areas, photographs and other elements.

The layout student will find experimental layout exceedingly helpful. Printed pictures cut from magazines can be used as a basis for constructing layout studies in areas of various shapes and sizes. Headlines and type masses may be rearranged and sketched in by hand. Thus, by reconstruction and comparison with original compositions a sense of relative values is gradually acquired.

There are many ingenious methods and procedures for attaining forceful, attention-compelling layouts, and as the student progresses he should study constantly the styles and techniques of the leading layout craftsmen. He should always remember that the successful layout man is the one who thoroughly evaluates all available materials and processes and utilizes them to their utmost.

Specialized art courses are available to those who strive for proficiency in illustration and other phases of art. To do reasonably professional-looking layouts, however, it generally suffices for the layout man to have a comprehensive working knowledge of art techniques and the ability to portray them adequately for presentation purposes.

Above are some typical layouts that forcefully convey the character of type and hand lettering.

The layout student can improve his technique in figure sketching by tracing examples from printed advertisements.

Here are some "befores" and "afters." The layout and the finished job often prove helpful in evaluating reproduction of a layout.

Single-stroke lettering with a ball-pointed pen or pencil is the simplest to draw.

The individual characteristics of the various lettering styles demand the use of pen points of suitable style and flexibility for fine lettering.

Some letterers prefer a well-pointed brush for certain styles of free-flowing lettering.

A flat brush is ideal for broad lettering.

The French curve may be used in formulating and perfecting curves in swash letters.

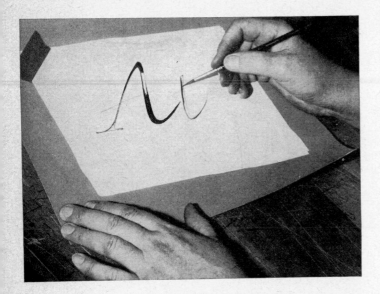

The copying of sound lettering styles from type specimen books is highly recommended.

The offset and gravure processes offer the layout man wide latitude in applying hand lettering.

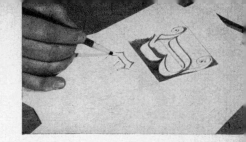

Fundamentals of Lettering

LETTERING ON A LAYOUT should be so well drawn that it expresses the character and feeling of the words it interprets, accentuates the typographical style, and accelerates the design construction of the composition. Fundamentally, this can be accomplished if one acquires a thorough understanding of the basic construction of lettering, the ability to clothe these structures with characterful surface rendering and the skill to compose them correctly. To attain the utmost proficiency in lettering, however, one must also possess a natural aptitude for artistic expression, inherent good taste in design, a steady trained hand and an eye for perfection in details.

The art of lettering being such a broad study, we must limit ourselves here to as much of its historical background, its influence on typographical design and its application in layout as serves the purpose of the beginner.

The fundamentals here set forth, combined with continued practice in copying from type specimen books and other sources of sound lettering styles, will aid the student in acquiring a lettering technique sufficient for average layout purposes.

Historical Background

A brief résumé of some historical aspects of lettering will give one a more intimate understanding of the various forms and functions of letters.

In seeking some means of visual communication, prehistoric man originated pictographs which he drew on the walls of a cave or on the stony side of a hill.

The Egyptians perfected the pictorial process by the introduction of hieroglyphics, a decorative form of picture writing, which was developed into a system of lettering symbols, each representing a word.

The Greeks, by adapting and elaborating the Egyptian hieroglyphics, eventually developed a crude original alphabet. It was named "Alpha-Beta" after the first two letters of their alphabet. This alphabet was composed of capitals only.

Throughout years of usage and refinement the Romans perfected the complete alphabet of Roman capitals, which is used to this day as the basis for all our standard letter forms. The lower case letters were a later development.

All of these alphabets originally were constructed of serif-less strokes. The Romans found in the development of chiseled inscriptions, however, that a sharper, more uniform termination could be given to the vertical strokes of capital letters by a horizontal right angle chisel cut, extending slightly beyond the width of the stroke and thus the serif was born. It also served the purpose of overcoming the tapered optical appearance of the upper parallel vertical outlines of letters. Gradually, curved serifs were developed which gave added grace and beauty to lettering.

The original Roman inscriptions at the base of the Trajan column in Rome, cut in the first century, still are used as unequalled samples of classical form and design.

Traditional lettering and type design of today, refined and elaborated through centuries of usage, differ little structurally from the ancient Roman design. The surface treatment of the various alphabets may vary but their fundamental structures remain unchanged.

As type designers of recent years have taken wide latitude in the creation of new styles to fit modern advertising techniques, so the medieval scribes elaborated and embellished the classical Roman design to meet utilitarian needs. They created the Gothic Text style which could be drawn with more flexibility with the quill and reed. Use of the Gothic Text style of lettering then became widespread and it was logical that Gutenberg should have copied this style in his first movable types.

The Gothic Text design influenced all subsequent typography until in later years a demand for more legibility prompted Jenson, Garamond, Caslon and other type designers to revert to the original Roman alphabet. The typographical reincarnation of the Roman style provided a more flexible means of expression in printing because of the many design advantages of this classical alphabet. It has since exerted its influence on all types of design and lettering.

Three Basic Lettering Styles

While letter styles are seemingly endless, any lettering style in the English language can be identified as being distinctly in one of the following structural categories: *Roman* (with italic), *Script and Gothic.*

Many contemporary styles may appear to defy classification but their fundamental structures stem primarily from one of these three styles or a combination of their main characteristics.

Roman Capitals

The twenty-six letters of the alphabet can be segregated into distinctive width and height groups. The purpose of this classification is to acquaint the lettering student with the measurements that control the structural design of each letter so that it will be harmoniously related to the others when composed in a line.

The following calculations, as are many other specifications for artistic construction, are variable to some degree in the hundreds of lettering styles, but it will be found that they are applicable in general to all letter forms that stem from the basic Roman construction.

The crossbar of the letter A, for example, may be moved higher or lower in certain alphabets to conform to the body weight of the letter. Likewise, the central horizontal bars of the letters E and F may be shortened or lengthened to serve specific design purposes.

Expanded or condensed styles are excluded from these calculations as they are distortions of the basic forms, and were designed to serve limited typographical purposes.

Using the dimensions of a perfect square as a basis for measurement, capital letters may be segregated into the following width categories:

Letters filling slightly *more* than the square in width— M and W

Letters filling the *entire* square in width— A V G O Q

Letters occupying about *three-quarters* of the square in width— C D U H N T X Y Z

Letters occupying *one-half* of the square in width— B E F J K L P R S

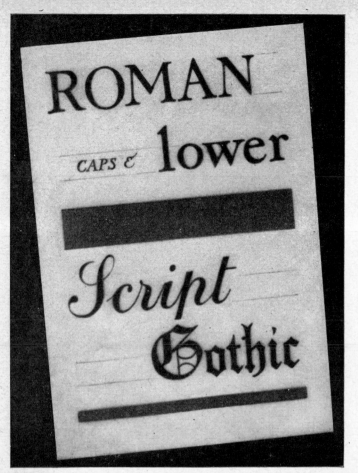

The three basic lettering styles are Roman (with italic), Script and Gothic Text.

The utmost expressibility in the variety of lettering techniques is graphically illustrated above.

A Gothic Text type in a layout that exemplifies the tradition of the form. This was the style of type Gutenberg used in printing his Bible. It harmonizes with deckle-edged, antique paper, Lombardic initials and colorful illumination. (*From the Eastern Series.*)

The above body type is known as "Uncial." It is symbolical of a lettering style of the early scribes. It evolved from the original Roman alphabet, becoming transformed by speed in writing. (*A Volk keepsake.*)

The space occupied by the letter I is dependent on its thickness and extent of serifs.

While it appears to the eye that all capital letters are of equal height, such is not the case.

Rounded parts of the letters C G J O Q S U and the apex or meeting points of the diagonals in the letters A V and W slightly exceed the top and bottom extremities of the square, to overcome the optical illusion of being smaller if drawn to fill the exact height of the square.

The letter Z is drawn a trifle less in height so it will not appear too full.

In the letters A E F H, the horizontal crossbars should be placed slightly above center to attain optical centering. Likewise, in the letter X the point of crossing of the diagonals should be drawn high center.

In the letter K, the diagonals should meet at a right angle and the apex should join the vertical at a high center point.

The letters B D P R are composed of semi-circular sweeps which gracefully blend into short horizontal strokes that join the verticals at right angles.

In the numerals the same general principles used in capitals prevail. Excluding the numeral 1, all the other nine characters occupy approximately the same width, generally about one-half the width of the square. In height, the rounded portions of 2 3 5 6 8 9 0 and the apex of 4 extend a trifle over the horizontals. This applies to all "modern" or lining figures. "Old style" figures are characterized by upward protrusion of the characters 6 and 8 and the lowering of 3 4 5 7 and 9 from the height of figures 1, 2 and 0.

Roman Lower Case

In comparison to the capitals, many more of the lower case letters are constructed with circular forms. Their curved contours contrast pleasantly with the angularity of the capitals.

Due to the varying lengths of ascenders and descenders in the many different alphabets, it is advisable to confine our calculations momentarily to the body or main portion of the letters.

41

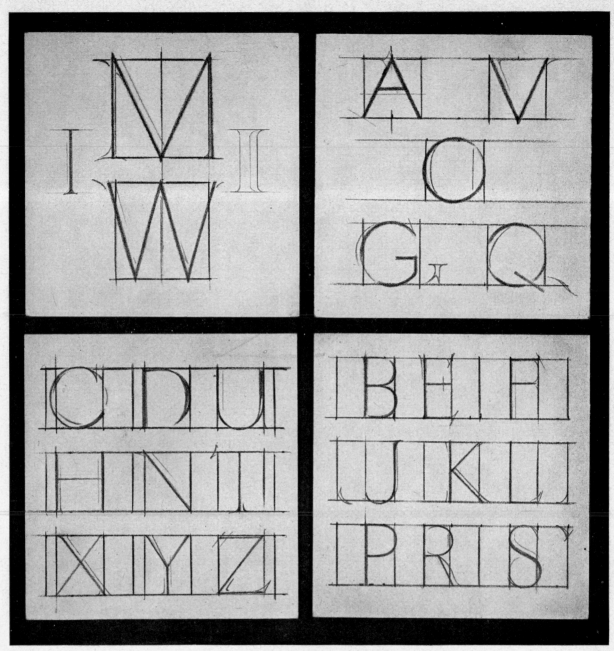

Capital letters are divided into 5 width groups. Top panel shows M and W occupying more than the full square in width; (right) A V G O Q occupy the full square; lower left shows the letters occupying approximately three-quarters of the square in width; letters in the last panel occupy approximately one-half the square width. The width of I is dependent on its style, as shown in top panel.

Lower case letters, likewise, are divided into width groups, using the main body for measurement. Top line shows m and w slightly wider than the square. Each of the center group of letters fills a full square. All letters in the bottom row occupy approximately three-quarters of the square width; the letters f t i j and l occupy space according to their style construction, as shown on top line.

Comparatively speaking, the height of the main body of lower case lettering is generally three-fifths of the capital height. Type designers usually divide the height of the entire type body, including ascenders and descenders, into seven parts. The capitals occupy the top five parts; the main body of the lower case the three central parts; the ascenders the two top parts and the descenders the two bottom parts.

As in capital forms, the letters m and w are approximately one-fourth wider than the square.

The bodies of the following letters, which are basically circular, fill a full square: a b c d e g o p q.

The following letters fill about an eighth less than the width of the square: h k n r s u v x y z.

The bodies of f and t being slightly more condensed occupy about one-half of the square.

The letter i and its companions j and l, fill space according to their vertical thickness.

Six of the lower case letters—s u v w x and z—retain the main distinguishing characteristics of the capitals.

The general rule that rounded letters or rounded portions of letters and the apex or meeting points of diagonals should exceed the horizontal extremities is applicable likewise to lower case. As in the capitals, the rounded body structures of such letters as c and o should occupy a slightly greater vertical area than normal letters such as i and x. Likewise, the angular portions of v and w should go below the bottom horizontal line.

In letters such as f and j, the curved parts should appear to spring from the verticals in a graceful curve. They should join the verticals at the junctions as the leaves of a plant stem gracefully from the body. They should have the appearance of sprouting gracefully from the verticals, rather than butting against them abruptly. Much of the grace and charm of the letter form can thus be retained.

The ascenders of the letters b d f h k l normally are aligned evenly at the top, but the letter t terminates approximately half way between this alignment and the top of the body of the lower case letters.

The descenders of the letters g j and y normally are aligned alike at the bottom, as are p and q.

Italics

Most every Roman type design has an italic counterpart. The italic font broadens the scope of the alphabet and is used for emphasis and contrast.

The italic font carries out the essential characteristics of the Roman in body structure, weight, contour, style of serif and other identifying characteristics. However, the vertical lines become diagonals slanting to the right and the anatomy of curved letters is redesigned accordingly. Most italic styles become more condensed in the transformation and assume an air of delicacy and momentum, as compared to the Roman.

Due to the innumerable styles of italic interpretations, it is practically suggested that one be guided generally by the comparative measurements outlined for Roman lettering, referring to specimen sheets of specific alphabets as occasion demands.

Script

Script styles simulate handwriting. Having no emphatic relation to the basic Roman alphabet, they should be used sparingly as their ornateness and delicacy limit their use to compositions of similar character.

The measurements of individual letters in script styles being far more variable than the Roman and italic, they are more difficult to classify. It is suggested, therefore, that the lettering student consult specimen books for guidance when lettering a specific script style.

In drawing script styles, as in the italic, one should maintain a uniform degree of slant in the lettering. The weight of the main body strokes and the thin connecting lines should be uniform and the contour and direction of the many curved elements should be harmonious.

Script should never be letter spaced and the letters should be tied together with the thin strokes so a continuous flow, similar to handwriting, is achieved.

The complete body height of the average letter may be divided into seven equal parts. All capitals, except J occupy the top five parts. The main portion of lower case letters occupies the three central parts, letters with ascenders occupy the five top parts; those with descenders, the five bottom parts. This drawing shows "built-up" lettering under construction.

The T-square and ruler may be used to form the basic construction of certain straight elements of lettering.

A uniform degree of slant in italic lettering may be maintained with the T-square held firmly at the proper angle to guide the triangle.

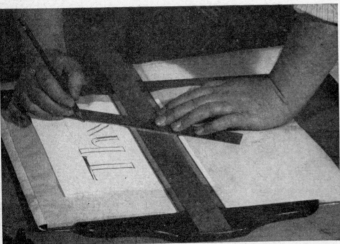

Characterful "built-up" lettering is achieved by careful allocation of each letter in light strokes and the gradual refinement and definition of contour by heavier strokes as correct placement is attained.

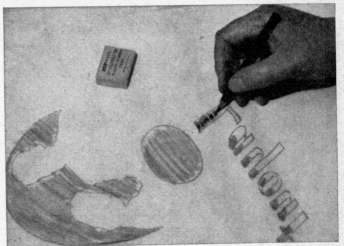

Colored crayons applied to the reverse side of a layout-tissue create a soft, pleasant pastel effect. The grayness of the tissue tones down the vividness of strong colors.

Gothic Text

The use of Gothic Text lettering is very limited in layout practice. However, the lettering student should familiarize himself with its main characteristics so that it may be utilized advantageously when occasion arises. Gothic Text lettering has a decided boldness in the main body structures, the verticals of which have curved or angular terminations, devoid of the conventional Roman style serifs. The vertical structures are connected with thinner angular strokes or curved sweeps, while the rounded structures taper from thin extremities to bold curves, which terminate abruptly at angular elements or graduate again to thin extremities.

The general structure of Gothic Text lettering simulates the thick and thin strokes of the easy-flowing hand lettering of the early scribes which was drawn with the quill and reed.

Again it is suggested that the lettering student consult specimen books when the use of Gothic Text is contemplated.

Spacing

The readability and pleasing appearance of lettering depends on correct spacing. No matter how skillful one may become in drawing individual letters, this ability is ineffective unless one can compose them harmoniously in a line or other grouping.

Correct spacing cannot be attained by applying the yardstick. It comes from the ability to place letters in such relation to each other that the optical appearance of the spacing is uniform and a free-flowing interpretation of the wording is attained.

Unharmonious spacing unnecessarily arrests the eye and disturbs the reader. Common examples are the wide gaps of white space commonly formed by letter combinations such as AT AV LA VA WO. These combinations must be equalized in relation to the balance of the lettering, either by a reduction of space between them or by letter spacing the other letters in the line.

Likewise, spacing between words should be optically uniform and adroitly allocated. Capital lines require more word spacing than lower case lines. In no case, however, should spacing cause unusually wide gaps anywhere to interrupt readability.

In roughing out lettering, the first crude division of the width allowed for the lettering should be done lightly. In going over the first roughout, try to give letters form and placement by gradually weighting their defin-ing lines. Heavy, definite strokes at the outset are visual barriers to re-shaping or shifting of characters.

One should not distort the structure or any detail of a letter to equalize spacing. Rather retain true proportions and shift letters in their entirety to right or left. Even color should be maintained in the thick and thin parts of lettering and the serifs should be drawn uniformly.

All lettering rendered in pencil, crayon or other medium that may smudge in handling should be protected by applying fixatif immediately on completion.

Review of Styles

The design possibilities of the thousands of lettering styles simulated in modern type designs are practically unlimited. From this assortment, the layout man can select a suitable style to fit almost any purpose, to harmonize with any treatment and to express any mood or characteristic.

Any one sound type style with its capitals, lower case, small capitals and italic forms, in light, medium and bold faces, has in itself a wide range of expressiveness. It is suggested, therefore, that one adhere to lettering that simulates a type style exclusively at the start rather than attempting to draw freehand lettering creations of his own.

Type founders have overcome most of the mechanical restrictions that formerly prevented exact duplication of certain lettering styles in type-casting and are constantly introducing fresh, novel designs. The specifica-tions of these type faces on layouts is generally to be recommended instead of the mediocre originations of the lettering beginner.

The beginner is particularly cautioned to avoid copying any of the distorted lettering styles prevalent in many of the books on "modern" lettering. They serve no useful layout purpose as they are impractical typo-

47

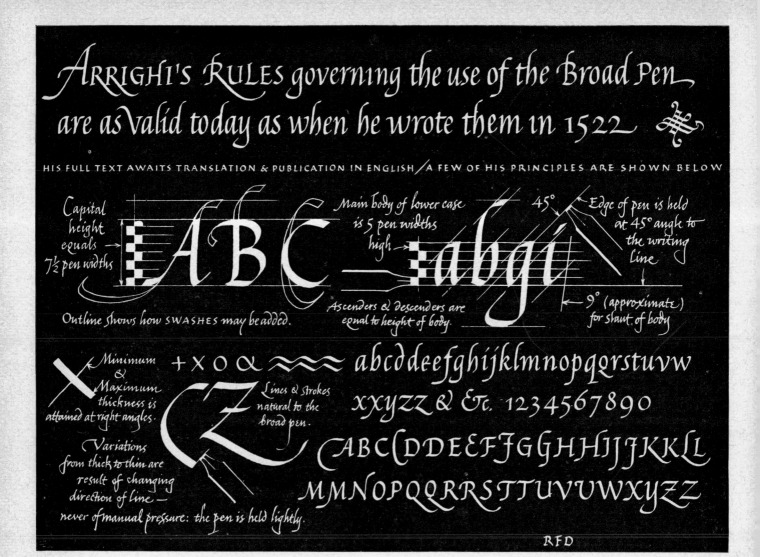

The achievement of the utmost freedom and originality in some forms of design may be attained only by the application of fine handwriting —calligraphy. It is with this thought in mind that we reproduce the above enlargement of a very instructive and interesting panel of the "Calligraphy" specimen sheet, left, of the Eastern series which graphically illustrates the use of the flat pen in calligraphy. It gives the proportionate height of caps and lower case, the degree of angle at which the pen should be held and other guidance for attaining graceful variations. The slant of the pen is never varied and the thick and thins are the result of changing the direction of line, never the pressure. This type of calligraphy was prevalent in the 16th century. Various italic styles of type are derivatives.

Designer of the Eastern Corp. two-color specimen sheet on calligraphy was Raymond F. DaBoll, nationally known Chicagoan, who is rated as one of this country's foremost calligraphers. Every character on the sheet, which in itself is a masterpiece of fine composition, is the work of Mr. DaBoll's facile pen.

Stanley Morison, eminent British typographer, defines calligraphy as follows:

"Calligraphy is the art of fine writing, communicated by agreed signs. If these signs or symbols are painted or engraved on wood or on stone, we have that extension of writing known as lettering, i.e., a large script formed with mechanical aids such as rules, compass and square. But it is the essence of handwriting that it be free from such but not all government, and of beautiful handwriting that it possess style. . . . Calligraphy may be defined as free hand in which the freedom is so nicely reconciled with order that the eye is pleased."

Reproduction courtesy of copyright owners, Eastern Corp.

graphically and costly to reproduce. Likewise, he should avoid adopting any of the modern theories that advocate complete revolutionizing of all traditional laws of design. For example, there are some who would eliminate capitals from our alphabet entirely.

People are influenced strongly by habit and custom. Any drastic deviation from traditionally accepted styles is not readily welcomed. The use of capital letters has received the approbation of typographers and artists for centuries, and the eye has been trained to accept these forms as correct.

There is too much structural effectiveness, beauty and design in our fundamental alphabet (all capitals) to sacrifice its use to a passing fad or fancy. True, lower case with its irregularity of line and contours pleasingly relieves monotony. In some display forms it is more readable than capitals and it is the logical choice for text areas. Full advantage should be taken of this legibility, but there is to the experienced designer a very evident lack of structural strength in an all lower case composition.

Lower case letters do not lend themselves well, except in rare instances, to letter spacing; and by their openness and irregularity disport themselves too freely to be controlled as well as capitals in constructing designs.

The advantage of using capitals in reverse plates, as structural bases in logotypes and trade-marks, and in achieving the utmost contrast and display emphasis when used with italics and other type forms, are evident in some of the illustrations throughout this volume.

Through years of continuous application and study, a deep appreciation for all design possibilities and limitations is acquired. The beginner is advised, however, to enter the study of lettering with an open mind. Eventually, by constantly solving problems as they arise he will evolve his own individuality and technique.

Top left panel shows that the basic construction of all Roman lettering is alike. The change in surface weight and contour, and the style of serif distinguishes a style. Top line in right panel further emphasizes the surface distinctions of various letter styles. The center line compares lining figures with old style figures. On the bottom line the alikeness of slope in italic lettering is emphasized. The incorrect and correct spacing of AVE is demonstrated. Lower left panel illustrates the optical rule which decrees that certain portions of letters must extend above or below the horizontal lineup so that all letters in a line will appear uniform in height. Lower right panel illustrates the surface transformations, possible also in the basic Roman lower case.

Thumbnails, Roughs, Visuals

THUMBNAILS are small fundamental sketches which are made to arrest basic layout ideas as they crystallize in the mind, and from which the actual-size layout will evolve.

These miniature sketches should be of an all-inclusive pattern, conveying the layout style and treatment without defining minute details.

As the name implies, thumbnails are drawn usually several square inches in area, in the same proportion as the anticipated actual-size layout. They are made with a medium lead pencil in a broad, sketchy treatment, usually on tracing paper.

As thumbnails are highly creative evolvements, no specific rules apply in their rendering. Some layout men carefully rule uniform areas and conform their designing thereto, while others swiftly sketch vague outlines which they may expand or contract proportionately as creative procedure suggests.

In the first light skeleton draft, the predominating display elements such as pictures, headlines, trade-marks, etc., are shaped and positioned in a phantomlike manner and text areas are faintly outlined. By working over this initial attempt with slightly heavier strokes, the elements may be enlarged, reduced, reshaped or repositioned; the groundwork given shape and the display elements correctly evaluated. Gradually, as the structure of the design is emphasized and tone values are added by still weightier strokes the composition develops and the layout idea takes definite form.

The amount of thumbnails necessary to arrive at a correct layout choice is problematical. Sometimes a few sketches will suffice, while at other times enough layout possibilities will prompt a dozen designs.

One should give vent to originality and enthusiasm and explore every idea to its utmost, but should not waste time with designs which do not crystallize spontaneously, or which seem too complicated or unpromising as they evolve. It is better to discard these efforts entirely and begin anew, always reconstructing, shifting or otherwise evaluating display elements.

Thumbnails used to develop a type layout for a magazine advertisement and the enlarged rough from which type was set. The selected layout is a combination of the two checked thumbnails in the lower right of the top panel. The pattern stems from the final thumbnail but is activated by the type style of the other. Note how the word "Pasigraphy" is accentuated and echoed by "Typography" in type similarity.

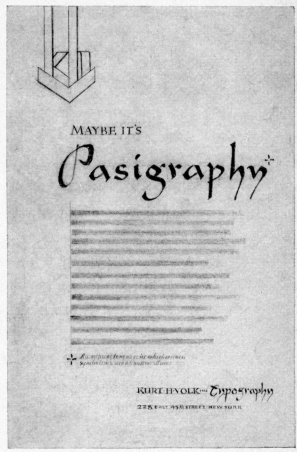

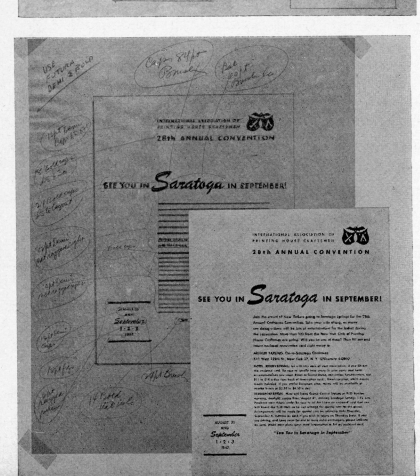

Left—An actual-size rough, explicitly marked for type styles, sizes, spacing and leading, facilitates composition and eliminates uncertainty. (All illustrations on this page considerably reduced from originals.)

When making thumbnails one should always keep the size and proportions of the eventual actual-size layout in mind together with a rough computation of the amount of text, otherwise these small sketches may lose their artistic casualness and practicability when enlarged. Areas that seem pleasing in thumbnails may not always conform typographically to the text on hand; pictures may not warrant the designated display values, or other shortcomings may influence the effectiveness of the enlarged layout, unless these eventualities have been anticipated.

The rendering of the average actual-size rough, while not requiring the artistic finesse of the presentation visual, should be basically correct in draughtsmanship and portray all design elements effectively.

A rough that explicitly defines specific type faces, correct spacing, margins, etc., imparts to the typesetter a sense of confidence and facilitates its mechanical reproduction. Likewise, if the type and cut areas have been calculated by a careful analysis of the manuscript and pictures the work of the makeup man is simplified.

Compositors may have widely divergent conceptions of layouts that are inaccurate or carelessly rendered, therefore, the more exact the layout, the more accurate will be the reproduction. Likewise, a rough that explicitly conveys the theme of a design to the artist, photographer, photoengraver and printer facilitates their workmanship and improves their product.

In the drawing of a visual, or artistically finished layout for presentation purposes, an actual-size rough may first be made on tracing tissue and transferred to the visual paper stock after all refinements have been made.

Photostats or photoprints of original photographs and drawings, scaled to proper sizes, are often pasted in position on visuals. Proofs of display type lines and small blocks of text type, likewise, may be added to help visualize the typographical treatment.

The particular purpose of every layout should be foremost in mind. For presentation purposes, the draughtsmanship of a visual should be painstakingly done. For strictly mechanical uses, roughs need not be artistically elegant but they should be precise and practical.

Suburban newspaper advertising can emulate the appearance of national advertising to the extent that layout and typographical techniques are applied. At left is a reduced reproduction of an institutional advertisement produced from a "velox" print of the dog's photograph and reproduction proofs of well chosen type, combined to the pattern of the accompanying tissue layout.

A complete line engraving results from the use of the "velox" which interprets the original photograph in a pattern of dots, on paper, similar to the engraver's halftone screen.

Warmest Greetings...

THE OFFICERS, DIRECTORS AND STAFF OF THIS INSTITUTION EXTEND THE WARMEST HOLIDAY GREETINGS TO ALL OUR MEMBERS AND FRIENDS.

...Our 60th Year...

Westfield Federal

SAVINGS *and Loan Association*

30 EAST BROAD, AT PROSPECT • WESTFIELD

WESTFIELD 2-4500

Westfield's Oldest Financial Institution

The reproduction above is from a line engraving made from the newspaper advertisement. The reduction brings the dots in the simulated halftone area closer together to resemble a fine screen halftone. A similar "line" method of reproduction was used many times in this volume, mainly to produce clean, sharp type presentations in combination with elements that were originally coarse screen halftones. It is well to consult your engraver, however, before such unusual techniques are employed.

Rough pencil layout by Henry Kopel for a trade paper advertisement with proof of the firm's logotype pasted at bottom.

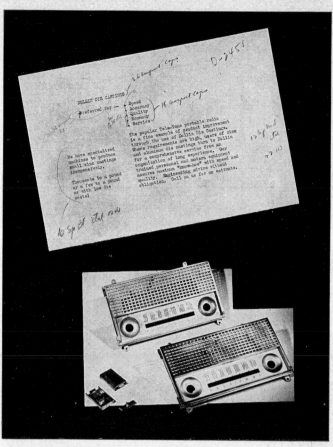

Typewritten copy, explicitly marked for typesetting, together with a photoprint of the products to be advertised.

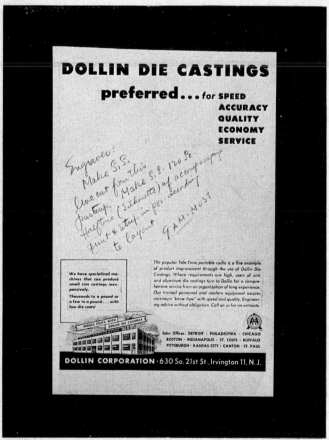

Reproduction proof of type, set to match layout, pasted up for an actual size line engraving. Note instructions to engraver.

Proof of the completed ad, a line engraving and a halftone combined as one plate, ready for printing or electrotyping.

Experimental pencil sketches in various lettering and type styles made to assist the client in formulating an attractive name pattern.

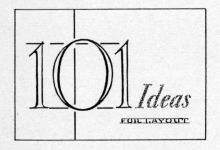

Roughs showing some of the many variations possible for placement of heading and pictorial elements using identical copy and art work.

Three booklet cover thumbnails in varying degrees of emphasis.

Analyzing the Copy

IN SEEKING INSPIRATION for a successful layout, one should pause long enough in the elementary analysis of copy and illustrative material to evaluate some very pertinent functional questions.

It may not seem esthetic to go commercial when formulating design, but the fact remains that the main purpose of advertising and printing is to sell something. And the client is primarily interested in results.

A successful layout man must not be merely a competent designer, he must also possess a diversified knowledge of human reactions and salesmanship of the highest order.

A thorough analysis of the following questions will aid materially in establishing an effective layout formula.

What are we trying to sell? Whom are we trying to interest? Through what medium and in what form can we best present the message?

If it is an advertisement in a newspaper or magazine, how much space will the layout require to tell the story effectively?

What about its position in relation to other advertising?

Is the layout to be designed for a left- or right-hand page? Has it an outside or inside column position? Is a horizontal shape more suitable than a vertical one?

Must the format for this and all future advertisements be alike in style and treatment or is this a "one time" insertion?

If the layout is for a direct mail piece, shall it take the form of a broadside, folder or pamphlet?

Does the nature of the message or the proper portrayal of the product require the use of color? Will color materially improve the illustrative values in pictures or art work?

What type of paper stock is to be used? Should it be colored, have an antique or coated surface? Will the anticipated size cut from standard paper sizes or will a special size or finish be economically feasible?

Right—A direct mail piece may take advantage of the many techniques of die-cutting, scoring, folding, collating and binding to increase its effectiveness. Here are some typical folders, broadsides, mailing cards and other formats.

What is the method of reproduction? What are the other mechanical requirements and limitations?

How about size and mailing weight to meet postage and budget limitation? Can it be a self-mailer? Should it enclose in a standard-size envelope or one of unusual size and color? Will a government postcard size suffice for a return mailing card?

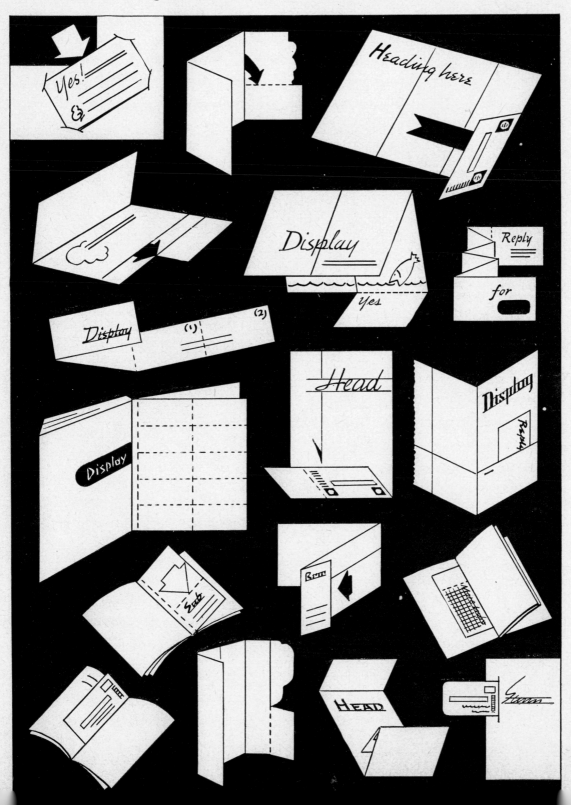

If it is a booklet, should it be a "self-cover" or clothed in a distinctive heavier stock? Can it be short-folded, die-cut or embossed to improve attention value? Will spot varnishing improve color appeal?

Besides these, there are still further elementary questions that must be considered. For instance:

Has the copy been reduced to the absolute minimum or can it be edited further to fit certain layout areas? Can liberty be taken with continuity to serve typographical expediencies? Must type alone tell the story —or may the layout suggest art work, hand lettering or photography?

How many pictures shall be used—which should predominate?

Has the client a type preference which must be respected?

Will the trade-mark or logotype fit the style of layout suggested or must it be changed in shape or tone, subdued or omitted entirely?

These are but some of the questions that may need to be answered before thumbnail sketches are begun. They present fundamental problems, the correct solution of which will materially influence the effectiveness of the layout.

"Should the shape be horizontal or vertical?" An elementary question which prompts evaluation of the copy in varying forms of display emphasis. This type of thumbnail rendering is worthy of presentation for client preference as to proportionate size and shape.

Below—a full-page vertical ad in a tabloid and its simultaneous interpretation as a horizontal half-page ad in a standard size newspaper.

Choosing the Layout Style

WHEN ONE CONSIDERS the wide range of layout treatments applicable to the advertising of furniture, food products, cosmetics, real estate, building equipment, clothing and other tangible items, and contrasts their specific appeal with that of such intangibles as insurance, travel, financial, political, organizational and institutional advertising, it becomes obvious that the selection of the correct layout style and treatment needs more than a perfunctory study.

It becomes apparent, likewise, that the layout style must not only interpret the character of the specific product or subject to be advertised, but it must also be designed to appeal to the type of audience it reaches.

Obviously, the primary question is whether to use a formal or an informal style. The chosen style must then be decisively accentuated or subtly restrained in both structural pattern and surface treatment according to the degree of emphasis required.

In formulating a layout for a tangible item, the layout man thoroughly analyzes the product and its trade-name; what its functions are; its origin and historical significance; its physical appearance; its label, package or identifying trade-mark; its specific appeal—dynamic or subtle, liberal or conservative, masculine or feminine—and evaluates the relative design importance of these factors.

Likewise, in a layout for an intangible subject, the main objective is the same—to discover some function, quality, characteristic or appeal from which the design may evolve, pictorially or typographically. One dramatizes the elements that are outstanding and subordinates those that are of less importance.

The layout pattern may suggest swift action, limited movement or definite repose. Likewise, it may suggest strength, conservatism, daintiness and innumerable other characteristics. Rugged, masculine compositions are sketched with strong, structural patterns, accentuated with decisive tone contrast; placid; reserved compositions with conservatively built struc-

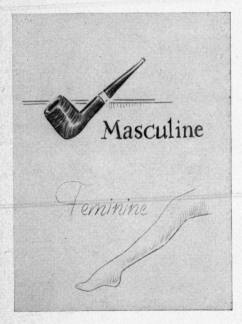

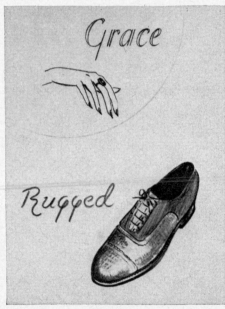

This forceful, dynamic formal layout exemplifies the strength of the plane and all it represents, by the ruggedness of hand lettering, art and typography.

Layout style may be accentuated by the physical construction, surface rendering, and style of lettering and typography. In each of the above examples the contrasting sketches symbolize the emphatic opposites. Strong masculine layouts require vigorous rendering of rugged patterns. Obviously, delicate, feminine patterns require lighter treatment.

Layout style may often be accentuated by subtle introduction of typical design vehicles and other easily recognized artistic mediums of expression that characterize periods, seasons, time, climate and vogues. They must be introduced adroitly and sparingly. Their presentation here is mainly to illustrate that the portrayal of habits, tastes, styles, customs and other physical properties create a subconscious reaction to layout style.

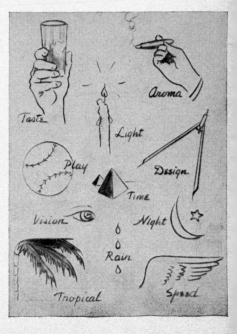

tures and more even-toned contrasts; dainty, feminine or ornate patterns with skeleton-like constructions and delicate surface treatments.

Layout style can be accentuated further by the treatment of pictorial elements. For example, a delicate woodcut or etching suggests antiquity and formality; a contrasty, bleed halftone or reverse plate typifies modernism and informality. Lettering and typographical techniques, likewise, can accentuate the layout style.

Size and shape of a layout area may indirectly influence layout style. For example, when limited copy and much white space prevail, as in a wide horizontal area, an informal, off-centered arrangement seems to suggest itself automatically. Besides activating the layout by dividing it into interesting patterns of space, an informal arrangement directs better attention to the display elements than if in a staid centered arrangement. A great amount of copy and a narrow deep vertical area, on the other hand, seem to suggest a more reserved, formal arrangement.

The decision to use an informal layout or the faster-moving tempo of informal layout, with its many variations and adaptations, should never be made arbitrarily. The divergence of taste and the unlimited possibilities for expressing one's creative ability should always prompt many experimental thumbnail sketches before definite conclusions are reached.

The main object is to achieve a layout that attracts attention, inspires favorable reaction, and reflects the character of the product or subject by the appropriateness of its graphic presentation.

The predominating central thumbnail above is immediately identified as a luxury steamship cruise folder by the sleek, trim ship symbol. Note how the graceful lines of the ship are accentuated by the "S" in the word "sunny." The musical symbol in the next left sketch is an obvious "eye-catcher" for those whose interest lies in that direction.

In the extreme left layout, the word "work" and a symbolic sketch of a factory are synonymous. The type style likewise matches the style of rendering in the illustration.

Santa Claus is but one symbol of Christmas. Santa's whiskers form an interesting panel for the message in the example above. The palm tree motif in the background of the last layout accentuates the copy in the panel in an appropriate manner. Here the more activated layout style is better suited to an italic heading.

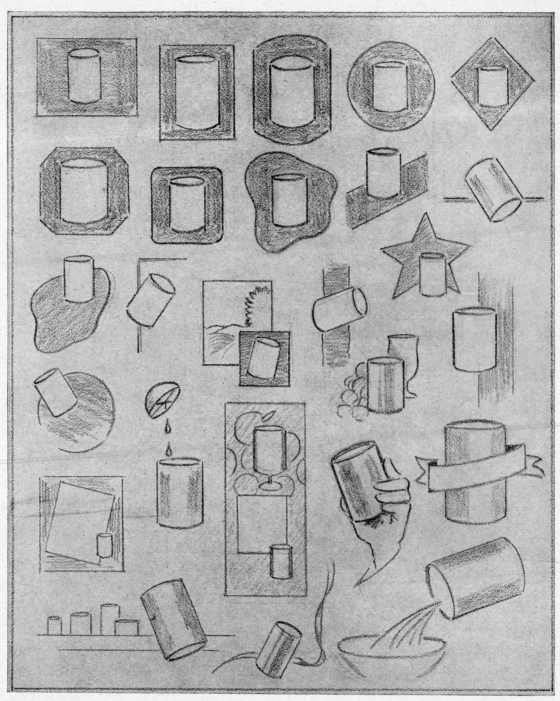

These experimental roughs illustrate the many possibilities for activating a simple object such as a can, in order to evaluate display importance. At first the can has a rectangular background which changes into various interesting shapes; the can then progressively becomes a silhouette in many changing positions with varying backgrounds, panels and borders, and then becomes an integral unit of a grouping with other elements or masses. The sketches showing juice dropping in the can and being emptied suggest utmost action. In the layout near the bottom center of the panel the can takes a subordinate reposeful position in relation to the other predominating elements such as a tempting glass of the juice, with fruit in the background to create atmosphere.

62

Evaluating Display Importance

BEFORE A DESIGN PATTERN is definitely formulated, the relative display importance of all units and masses must be established. The display unit that is to predominate must be selected and the attention values of the remaining units correctly evaluated. The purpose of this procedure is to formulate a logical display continuity and proper visual sequence in the layout.

It is obvious that if the display values of units are weak and unemphatic, monotony prevails and the visual progression is indecisive. Likewise, if display values of units are overemphasized they will attract undue attention to themselves and cause confusion.

The experienced layout man intuitively analyzes a layout problem as it arises and accentuates display importance by skillfully sizing, shaping and positioning the units and carefully regulating their tones.

The layout student must develop this ability by acquiring an appreciation for the many intangible display qualities in pictures and pictorial compositions; the expressiveness and movement of shapes and tones; the subtle characteristics of lettering, typography and ornamentation; and the endless possibilities in space divisioning and allocation.

In a typographical layout, the initial objective is to "break down" copy into forceful display units and text masses that will emphasize the important points of the message in logical order. This analytical process is one of the most essential in establishing display importance.

Words as they are spoken can be accentuated by tone of voice and change of pace in their delivery. The printed word, likewise, needs visual emphasis and accentuation to make it effective and the different letter forms, such as capitals, small capitals, lower case and italics, in a wide variety of display patterns may be employed for this purpose.

The proficient layout man thoroughly evaluates every phase of the display copy at hand. He roughly analyzes the construction of headlines and subheads and transforms them into properly contrasting typographical pat-

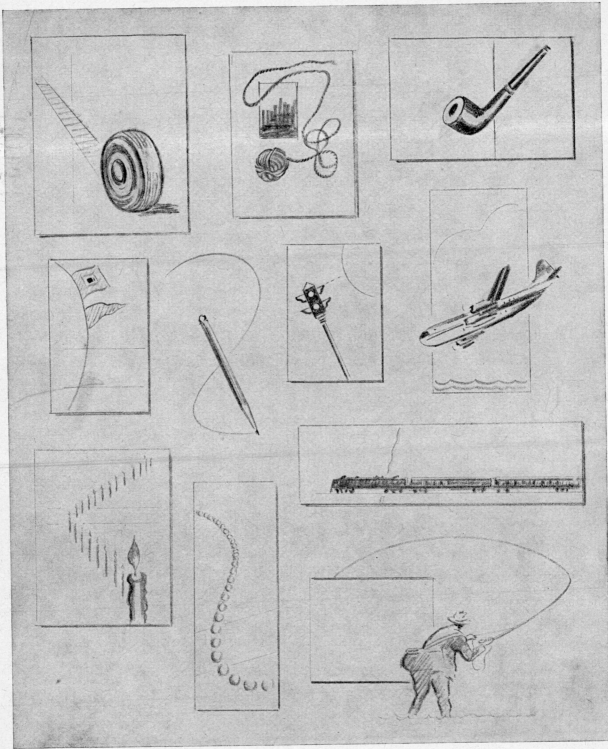

The expressiveness and movement of shapes and the directional qualities in pictures and compositions are hereby illustrated. The many display qualities of objects become apparent when activated in small experimental thumbnails as shown. In the first sketch, depth and perspective is emphasized, and the tire gets prime attention in the foreground. In the rough to its right, the ball of yarn interestingly brings the eye to the rectangular picture. The other roughs show interest being directed and space divided by functional elements.

terns. Likewise, he studies the text matter and transforms it into experimental type masses of various sizes, shapes and tones, choosing those that can best be combined with the other display elements.

Pictures may serve as predominating display units; as backgrounds or other ingenious design devices for varying degrees of typographical display; or as subtle, subordinate elements according to their relative importance in a layout.

Where there are a number of pictorial elements in a layout that have similar importance, they should be grouped together and their collective display value appraised as one. Thus, by reducing the number of elements, evaluation of display importance is simplified and the design procedure facilitated. This technique is likewise applicable to type units and masses, lettering and other elements that are related.

Below—Preliminary "breaking down" of the copy to achieve the proper degree of emphasis and pattern is done roughly at first. When the form is acceptable, exact type style, tone, size and spacing are later refinements.

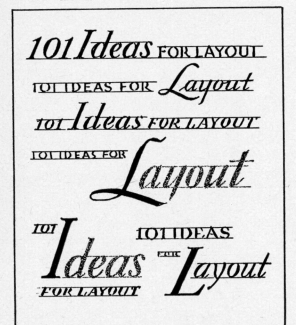

Four experimental roughs to decide another elementary question—
"which should predominate, the product, slogan or trade-mark?"
The left layouts show the product and trade-mark predominating;
the right layouts subordinate the product to the display copy.

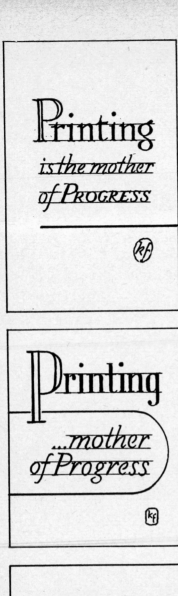

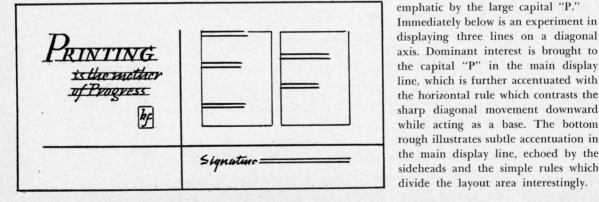

Proper choice of type sizes, structural forms, weights and the manner in which they are composed are essential factors in typographical accentuation. One chooses the most important textual element for display emphasis and, by contrasting it in size, shape, tone and position, sets it apart in some manner from the remaining "copy." Choosing next the element that is of secondary importance, one likewise emphasizes it in due relationship. This procedure continues until all elements have been properly evaluated. To fully achieve good accentuation, one must ever be conscious of the axiom, "All display is no display," and thus, by restraint in size, maintain the elements of lesser importance in proper relationship.

The seven sketches at the left are varying interpretations of the same basic copy. Occasional omission of words such as "of" or "the" permits better display emphasis.

The top left thumbnail emphasizes "Printing" predominantly, while giving secondary importance to "Progress." The rule helps maintain balance by its directional movement to the right to counterbalance the weight of the large initial at top.

The example directly beneath utilizes a large capital and the lines of the panel to divide space interestingly and unify the three lines of display.

The third example below utilizes an unusual arrangement of four type sizes to achieve contrast and ties in the entire word "Progress" with the capital "P" in "Printing" for emphasis.

In the top right sketch, a deep vertical band on which the capital "P" is reversed "keys" the vertical movement of the layout pattern, which is contrasted in movement by the two horizontal lines. The capital "P" in "Progress" is just strong enough to emphasize this word and "echo" the large vertical panel.

The basically formal arrangement in the next thumbnail below is made more emphatic by the large capital "P."

Immediately below is an experiment in displaying three lines on a diagonal axis. Dominant interest is brought to the capital "P" in the main display line, which is further accentuated with the horizontal rule which contrasts the sharp diagonal movement downward while acting as a base. The bottom rough illustrates subtle accentuation in the main display line, echoed by the sideheads and the simple rules which divide the layout area interestingly.

Basic Design Requisites PART FOUR

PREVIOUS CHAPTERS were designed to inculcate an understanding of the purpose and scope of layout, the many factors that influence the choice of format and layout style and the fundamentals for applying materials and techniques.

Our study progresses now to an evaluation of the five basic design requisites for a successful layout, whether it be a thumbnail sketch, an actual-size rough or an elaborately drawn visual.

These basic design requisites are *proportion, balance, contrast, rhythm* and *unity*.

Their functions in layout are predicated on the basic principle that certain harmonious combinations of shapes, masses and tones create favorable impressions on the mind, while groups of unrelated and unharmonious elements produce unpleasant reactions.

While definite mathematical calculations may be applicable to architecture and certain other arts, the planning of contemporary advertising and printing is such a widely variable creative process that it is inadvisable to advocate rigid rules for applying the basic design requisites. Rather, one should acquire a sound fundamental understanding of the basic purpose of each design requisite and the principles which govern its application.

Success in layout is achieved mainly by establishing in the mind a diversified vocabulary of sound design formulae, effective construction patterns and successfully tried procedures.

How to position a display unit correctly and how to regulate its size, shape and tone effectively depends on a sense of correctness and good taste developed by experience rather than by rules and measurements.

Proportion

An object is said to be well-proportioned if its shape is optically interesting, its structural parts harmoniously related yet not monotonous in size, and the whole a combination of the artistic and the useful.

67

In nature, there is much evidence of such structural harmony. Trees and plants, stars and planets, the human body itself—all are examples of good proportion.

Being influenced by a naturally developed sense of correct proportion, the eye reacts favorably to layouts that are well-proportioned and rejects those which have mathematically obvious dimensions or which place together unrelated sizes and shapes.

In an absolute square, the four equal sides may be said to be harmoniously related, but the area is static, monotonous and uninteresting because the eye quickly perceives the equality of dimensions. Likewise, any rectangular shape is inartistically proportioned if one dimension is an easily recognized multiple of the other.

It is obvious then, that the basic rule for attaining correct proportion is to regulate the dimensions of the area or object so that the eye does not readily fathom the mathematical relation of its measurements.

The page sizes of standard newspapers and magazines as a rule are correctly proportioned. However, certain space allocations therein are often badly proportioned, and when this design handicap prevails, the height or width of the layout area should be reduced optically. Rules, Ben Day borders, panels, ornamentation and many other ingenious devices may be utilized to secure a better proportioned area.

Good proportion is more readily accomplished in the design of direct mail and other individually printed advertising because of wider latitude in size and shape of layout area.

In the planning of folders, booklets and pamphlets the use of unusual folds, die cutting and other devices are often used to improve proportion.

All possibilities should be explored to achieve an interesting, well-proportioned layout area at the outset. Having accomplished this, the units and masses within the area should be sized, shaped and positioned to conform harmoniously to the area.

Initial outlines of units and masses should be penciled faintly to obtain an experimental allocation of elements. These outlines should be emphasized gradually with heavier strokes as correct proportion is achieved.

In this panel are shown paired examples of how static areas and monotonous space divisions may be improved in interest by changing mathematically obvious dimensions.

The uninteresting square at top left becomes a better proportioned and more pleasing area by reducing its height, as shown at its right.

The next two pairings directly beneath demonstrate how both areas, and space patterns within areas, may be improved by altering dimensions so that the eye does not readily perceive their mathematical relationship.

The two patterns at extreme lower left illustrate two ways of improving the double square directly above them.

At top right, the four pairings show basic examples of how proportion is improved in horizontal patterns by interesting rectangular and diagonal divisions.

The four groupings at lower right illustrate how angular and circular areas may be more interestingly proportioned and divided.

Above, at left, is rough tissue layout of two inside pages of a folder which by natural fold are alike in dimensions. The display lines are well regulated in size, width and placement to divide the layout area into an interesting pattern inside of Franklin's profile. The text masses are varied in size, while maintaining proportionate relationship. Note, however, how much more effective the finished printed piece becomes when the left side is reduced by die-cutting it to conform to the right-hand background pattern.

Skillful placement of initial letters, rules, ornaments, type lines and masses divides an area into lively, activated areas.

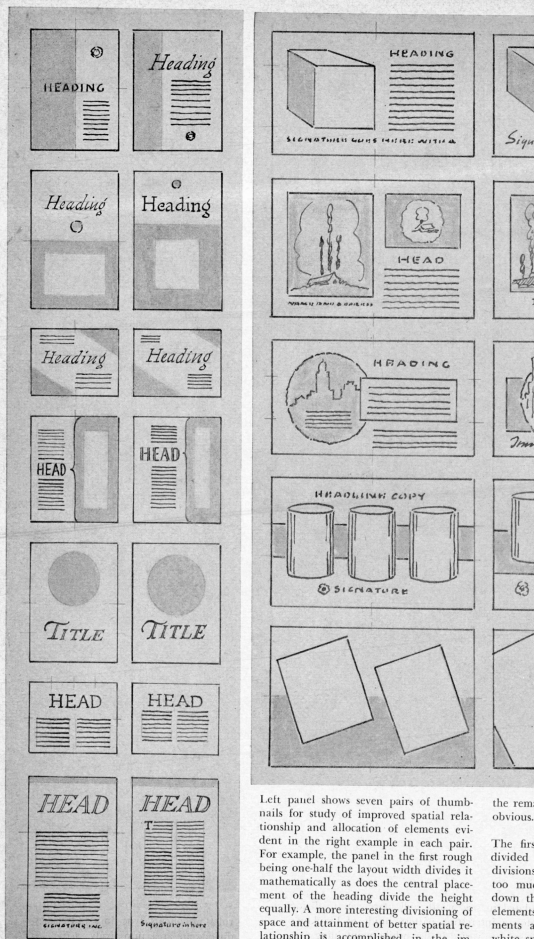

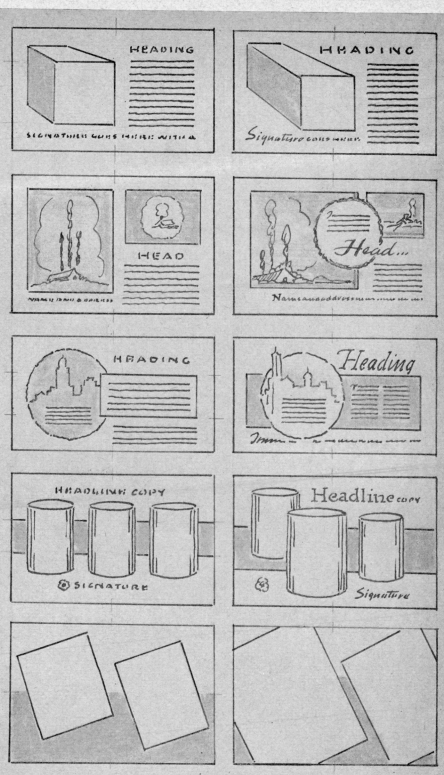

Left panel shows seven pairs of thumbnails for study of improved spatial relationship and allocation of elements evident in the right example in each pair. For example, the panel in the first rough being one-half the layout width divides it mathematically as does the central placement of the heading divide the height equally. A more interesting divisioning of space and attainment of better spatial relationship is accomplished in the improved thumbnail at top right. By changing size, shape and position of elements in

the remainder of thumbnails the result is obvious.

The first thumbnail in panel above is divided into two static and uninteresting divisions because left and right areas are too much alike in width. White space down the center also helps separate the elements. By changing the widths of elements a more interesting allocation of white space is attained. The other pairs likewise show improvement when spatial divisioning is not done mathematically.

However, before the final emphatic strokes accentuate the definite contour and position of the units and masses one should again evaluate thoroughly their size and shape harmony.

Variety in size and shape of units and masses should be accomplished without sacrifice of underlying relationships. Shapes whose dimensions are too extreme and unrelated should be avoided.

Balance

As the eye reacts favorably to well-proportioned areas, units and masses, it likewise is impressed by layouts in which these units are composed in harmonious balance.

Balance is one of Nature's most fundamental laws. It is defined as repose, resulting from the equilibrium of equal weights, or of unequal weights placed in properly balanced positions.

In early childhood we learn the significance of attaining balance in our movements, and as we subconsciously observe the proper distribution of weight in the objects of nature, we gradually develop a sense of optical balance. It is logical then, that we prefer layout compositions that are harmoniously balanced rather than those that are not.

In a layout, balance is attained by carefully regulating the size, shape, tone and position of the units in relation to the optical center of the area.

To be optically balanced, a composition of units need not be of a formal or centered arrangement, but units and masses should be so positioned that the entire composition appears naturally balanced in the layout area with the optical center as a pivot.

The optical center should be used because if a composition evolves from the exact mathematical center, the composition will always appear low to the eye and seem unbalanced vertically.

The basic principle for maintaining balance in a layout can best be illustrated by the following example: Assume that two rectangular units of equal size and tone are balanced on the central pivot. If one is enlarged in size, its tonal weight must be reduced to retain its optical balance. Likewise, if one is reduced in size its tonal weight must be increased to main-

71

tain balance. If either is moved to right or left, its size or tone must be regulated according to its relative position from the pivotal point. Thus, fundamentally, by the control of size, tone and position of units, balance is regulated.

The shape of units also must be considered, as irregularly shaped units such as silhouettes, vignettes and the like, exert more influence on the eye than do rectangular units and therefore may be said to be of greater weight.

The mechanics for controlling the tone of units lie in regulating tonal values in art work, photography, lettering, screen tints and reverse plates; composing type areas of varying weights and sizes; and spacing type lines and masses to achieve definite tonal patterns.

As successful balance in layout stems mainly from an inherent sense of balance, developed by constant study and application, it is essential that the layout student never cease his experiments in attaining optical balance.

Experimenting with cutouts of black and various shades of gray cover stock, placing them in a given area, shifting, cropping and manipulating them to evaluate results in balance, will inculcate a sense of size, shape, tone and position values.

Likewise, other factors such as margins, space divisions and allocation of white space may thus be evaluated. They assist materially in maintaining balance when applied correctly.

Balance in a layout is often upset by details that are seemingly inconsequential, such as an initial letter that is of improper weight, unorthodox shape or in a freakish position; a photograph whose cropping calls undue attention to detracting elements and values therein; hand lettering or typography that is of freakish construction; text masses that have too many accentuations, indentations and irregular lines; improperly chosen values in reverse and screen plates. These are a few of the unfavorable elements that can destroy the equilibrium of a layout that appeared structurally balanced at the beginning.

Obviously, then, the layout man must not only concern himself with the major obvious factors that influence optical balance, but he must control all minute details that affect the equilibrium of a layout.

Contrast

Contrast is that quality in a layout which imparts life, sparkle, variety and emphasis to a composition. It eliminates monotony and accentuates display values.

As similarity of dimensions is to be avoided to attain correct proportion so is monotonous similarity in size, shape, tone and direction of units incongruous to good contrast. Proper contrast is achieved by subordinating inconsequential elements and giving display emphasis to the more important units.

The ideal layout is one in which one specific display element predominates. That element may be a picture, headline, trade-mark or slogan.

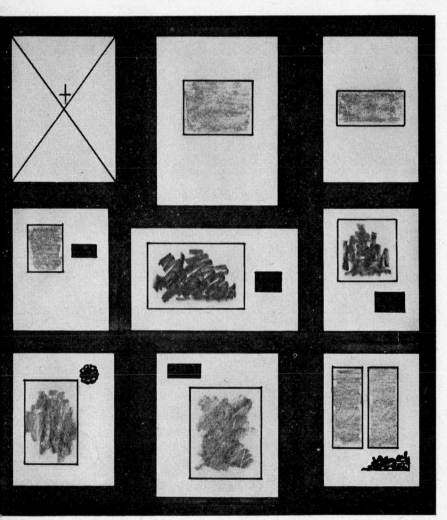

The cross in the first example in this panel shows the approximate position of the optical center, somewhat above the mathematical center. The next example places an element approximately in the optical center, while the third illustrates that an element appears too low and unbalanced vertically when in exact center.

The remainder of the experimental sketches illustrates the principle that when elements are unequal in size, optical balance must be maintained by regulating shape, tone and position of elements in relation to the optical center.

Circular shapes exert more attraction than do similarly toned rectangular shapes of approximate size; likewise, irregularly shaped objects attract the eye more than either and must be skillfully placed to maintain optical balance.

Black and white are the utmost in contrast, but more interest is created when intermediate tones of gray are added. The above panel is an experimental pasteup of paper to evaluate the principle.

While monotony of height and width of display units is to be avoided, variety of sizes and shapes must be limited as overemphatic contrast defeats its purpose and results in a spotty, discordant layout.

Restraint should be used in the number of display type sizes and contrast should be attained by fullest use of capitals, small capitals, lower case and italics in each font.

Contrast in width of display lines can be controlled by proper divisioning of copy and the correct introduction of letter spacing, word spacing and other typographical expedients.

In a group of pictures, one may be enlarged slightly to serve as a contrasting element to the others but its size should be restrained so that relative proportions are maintained.

Contrast in shape should be achieved without effecting too many unrelated, irregularly shaped elements, Rectangular masses should predominate over odd shapes such as silhouettes, vignettes, ovals and circles, which should be used sparingly.

Again we advocate the practice of cutting rectangular and irregularly shaped elements in black, white and the various tones of gray paper, for experiments in contrast of size, shape, tone and position.

Black and white creates the sharpest tonal contrast, but the most interesting compositions are those that contain the two in combination with limited intermediary gray tones.

Some of the simple mechanics for achieving contrast in tone are: balancing strong display lines against lighter-toned text masses; placing black reverse areas against screens of various gray tones; reducing or intensifying values in halftones and placing these contrasting tones in striking emphasis; superimposing properly accentuated type with contrasting values of illustrations, toned backgrounds, ornamentation, rules and borders; skillfully controlling the tonal values in text areas by proper selection of type weight, spacing and leading.

As in the shaping of elements, contrast in tone likewise must be carefully controlled as too many tonal values are apt to cause a spotty, jumpy appearance, confuse the eye and divert attention incorrectly.

Contrast in direction is achieved by regulating the shape of units and masses. The eye follows the vertical shape of a cut, rule or text mass downward, a horizontal mass to left or right, an initial letter in the direction of its slope and an irregular shape to the point of interest it best emphasizes. Thus contrast in shape can be utilized to carry the eye in the desired direction, to visualize all elements in their proper order.

Two display elements of monotonous alikeness in size, shape and tone are uninteresting. Examples at left show how contrast is achieved by emphatically enlarging one element and reducing the tone value of the other. The bottom examples illustrate the same basic principle and also how their overlapping increases contrast and creates unity.

The size, shape, tone and position of all elements influence the visual sequence. The diagrammatic sketches below evaluate contrast in direction, as outlined in text above.

The two areas in the first panel at left may be visualized as text masses, pictures, tint backgrounds for type, or other elements in a layout. At the right utmost contrast has been created by emphasizing size, shape, tone and position of the predominating element.

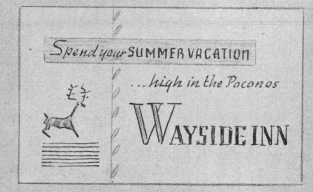

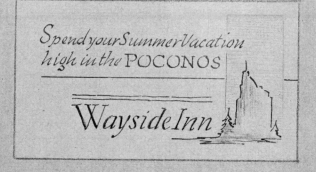

Various degrees of display emphasis are illustrated in the experimental thumbnails above. Sometimes the contrast is very emphatic while in some cases it is more subtle. By employing the full range of type forms in harmonious groupings and utilizing lettering, pictorial elements and suitable ornamentation in proper emphasis, the layout function of attracting the eye is facilitated.

The technique in the thumbnail below adds "punch" and typifies a poster-type layout while the roughs above are more restrained. Bottom right illustrates some of the mediums employed in rendering these thumbnails.

Rhythm

In a composition of poetry or music, rhythm is the medium that imparts action, variety and interest, by measuring and balancing the movement of sound. In layout, likewise, rhythm is the medium that instills action, variety and interest, by measuring and balancing the movement of vision. Rhythm in layout should give expression to the theme of the subject. It may be slow, fast or intermediate, according to the tempo desired. Obviously, the mechanics of movement must vary accordingly.

In a composition the eye is attracted naturally to the display element that is in the most dominant position or has the greatest attention value. It then progresses according to the visual sequence of the remaining elements, either completing the cycle of the layout pattern effectively or becoming confused and losing interest. It is logical that if the size, shape, tone and position of every element is regulated correctly, the design flow of the layout is facilitated and the eye is carried throughout in a logical progression. The natural direction of reading is from left to right, from top to bottom, from top left of a page to the right bottom. A design that leads the eye from the upper left of a composition, through all elements, to a successful terminus at the lower right accomplishes its purpose in a most logical manner. That is not to say, however, that every design must follow this procedure.

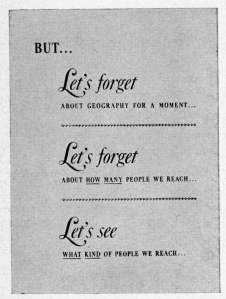  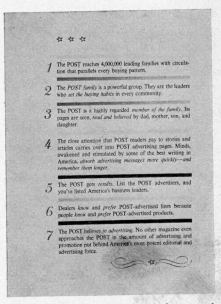

These three examples illustrate how rhythm may be stimulated in all-type presentations. In the left layout, rhythm is accelerated by repetition of large initials in color. The decorative border in color then relieves the eye by its horizontal movement. The center layout, by the setting of type flush left on a vertical axis, irregular at the right, promotes downward vertical rhythm. The design also promotes rhythm by repetition of similarly shaped display lines properly emphasized. The right layout is activated by numerical sequence of figures which are alike in style, and repetition of bands and text masses.

The decided rhythmic movement in the layout at the left is accomplished by the repetition of similar, yet contrastingly smaller, units placed in proper optical sequence. The eye is led from top left to bottom right, thence by the rules to the element at the left. In the right layout, rhythm is stimulated by directional movement of display lettering, illustration and reverse panel at bottom.

A design may evolve from many different points in the layout area, and the design flow may be interpreted by a variety of patterns, but it is well for the layout student to adopt practices which conform with basic optical procedures and allow the unusual and more complicated layout processes to evolve from later experiences.

One controls the visionary direction of units or masses by sizing and shaping them to properly accentuate the design qualities of their elements; also by proper toning and positioning. For example, a vertically shaped element directs attention downward or upward, a horizontal element to either right or left and an angular, circular or other irregular element in the direction of its influencing characteristics.

The direction of a narrow horizontal mass can be changed by placing near its terminus, a vertical mass, trade-mark, ornament, initial letter or other element that will lead the eye in the direction suggested by the added element.

The monotonous rhythm of identical, deep vertical masses can be interrupted by placing a narrow horizontal element across the bottom margin to relieve the continuous downward movement and create interest by changing optical direction.

The attention value of smaller elements may be increased over larger ones by emphasizing their tonal values, altering them to effect unusual, irregular shapes and by surrounding them with large white areas. Thus, by utilizing the influence of another basic layout requisite—contrast—rhythm can be accentuated.

Contrast should prevent monotony but must not be overemphasized. For example, a repetition of many uniform elements or masses can be skillfully accentuated by changing certain logical elements in size, shape, tone or position. However, if any element is overemphasized, disorder will prevail and the correct movement of vision will be upset.

Unity

Casually glancing at a tree, whose elements are normal and properly grouped, we comprehend it as one unified object. We do not visualize each individual leaf, twig or branch. Likewise, with an architecturally correct building, our immediate attention is not drawn to doors, windows or other structural elements, but all are assimilated as one unified structure. In each instance, correct grouping together of well-proportioned essential elements combines them into a harmonious unit.

A layout, likewise, should be constructed so that its component parts are harmoniously combined and it is comprehended at first glance as one unified composition.

As the incorrect shaping and placing of windows, doors or other structural elements may affect the unified appearance of a building, by calling undue attention to these units, so may the unharmonious shaping and placing of units and masses in a layout disturb the unity so essential to secure concerted attention and interest.

Unity holds a design together. It prevents looseness and disorder when a number of variable units and masses must be combined in a layout. The fundamental objective is to simplify the number, shapes, sizes and positions of display units by grouping them in an orderly, unified composition.

In an all-type presentation, this simplification is primarily achieved by careful analysis of the copy for the purpose of grouping all related text, eliminating all unnecessary paragraphing, indentions and other unimportant accentuations in type sizes, styles and measures. When the copy has been segregated into a minimum number of masses, the problem of unifying them in a composition is simplified.

When illustrations, type and other elements are combined, the same

Russeks
Manufacturing Furriers

Our Natural Ranch Mink **Paletot** and **Muff**, with tiers of horizontally worked skins $1500

Our White Russian Ermine **Tippet**, its capelet fringed with ermine tails . . $1500

Our Black Persian **Pelerine**, with the silky fringe of tassels . . . $500

Our Leopard **Stole**, lined and faced with rich scarlet wool $650

Our Black Persian Tiered **Palatine** and **Muff**, of the frog fastening . . . $500

Our Natural Wild Mink **Cape Stole**, of the diagonally worked skins . . . $2500

"Little" Furs by
Russeks Design Studio . . .

...paletots, capes, stoles, pelerines, muffs...that revive the mode of Grandmother's day in a new, Paris-inspired feeling for Fall. Exquisitely interpreted by our own Ralph Marano...and exactingly created here in our workrooms on the premises. From a new collection of "little" furs found only at Russeks, priced from $500 to $2500

Design Studio—Main Floor

Subject to 20% Federal Tax

Russeks New York · Brooklyn Chicago

Completely Air-Conditioned

On opposite page is a reduction of a full-page newspaper ad which typifies *rhythm* by placement of similarly-shaped pictorial elements in a dynamic, rhythmic pattern. The type is Bernhard Modern.

The reduced three- and two-column ads at the right employ the basic design requisites of sound *proportion*, subtle *balance* and effective *contrast*, *unified* in a fast-moving *rhythmic* pattern. These ads are newspaper-set, in Condensed Gothic and Sans Serif types.

The McAlpin ad, below, also utilizes similarly-shaped typographical elements to introduce *rhythm* in the layout. Both layouts exemplify *unity* by overlapping of rhythmic elements. The Sans Serif types accentuate the simplicity of pattern and art rendering.

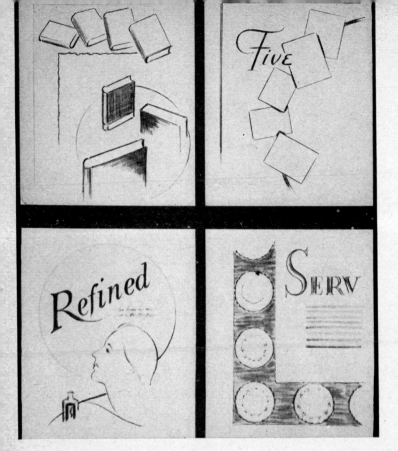

Examples of unity, achieved by co-ordinating related elements by the use of borders, panels and backgrounds. In the layout at left bottom the circular background unifies heading, subhead, picture and product in one subtle grouping.

Simple sketches of newspaper ads showing how objects may be unified by means of decorative devices, background panels, overlapping of pictures and by rule boxes. Thus display elements are reduced to a minimum.

fundamentals are applicable. Individual display units that have a common interest and are of equal importance should be grouped together and the design importance of the collective group should be evaluated as a unit.

There are many techniques for arranging related illustrations in orderly combinations. They may be grouped to form one pictorial element, alone or in conjunction with related type masses, with Ben Day backgrounds, screen panels or borders. They may be combined in a panel down the side, across the top of a page, diagonally or in other orderly succession. Combining a trade-mark with a signature, address and other related copy accomplishes the same objective. These are but a few examples of rudimentary procedures for attaining unity.

Of all design requisites, unity is of the greatest importance, for if we achieve *proportion* and *balance, contrast* and *rhythm,* and fail in the combining of all into a unified and harmonious composition, attention-value is scattered and interest is disintegrated.

The top left thumbnail illustrates the monotony in size and shape that prevails when two elements that are so alike are composed in a layout. They fight for attention, with neither predominating. The corrected version at right contrasts a larger vertical area against a smaller horizontal element, and thus contrast is achieved.

Directly beneath, the left thumbnail is unbalanced but suffers primarily because the solid margins around the white panel are too uniform. The better distribution of weight through a non-mathematical alikeness of margins improves the right layout.

In the third from top, left, the vertical division of space is uniform, which, while permissible in a strictly formal layout such as this, may become more activated and interesting, as in the right version.

In the left minature directly beneath, the horizontal division of space is likewise too uniform, and so are the resultant panels, while the element at the bottom is ineffective in shape. The revised layout definitely contrasts shapes and sizes and promotes depth and unity by accentuating the bottom element against the intermediary gray tone of the panel, which acts as the unifying element of the whole layout.

The bottom left layout area is too mechanically divided in width with the upper and lower vertical lines of the arrow, and its right point divides the height in half. By changing the shape of the arrow a less monotonous color pattern is achieved.

The two top right examples show (left) how two letters of equal size are equally attractive to the eye. By increasing the "A" in the right layout, it dominates the layout effectively.

Immediately below, the left layout shows how a solid band (again mathematically dividing a horizontal area) can predominate a pattern so that other elements will be too insignificant unless their display value is accentuated, as in the right revised thumbnail. Note that the tone has been diminished at the bottom to maintain relative tone harmony with the other elements which have been placed at upper left and bottom right respectively to enliven the pattern. Balance is maintained by accentuating a "shadow" rule at the right side with the suggested emblem to counterbalance the "50" at the left.

The first of the three examples directly beneath displays a squared element which is too nearly alike in size to the silhouetted element to be effective. The two revised examples to the right forcefully contrast size, shape and tone in a more emphatic way. Directly below, the three circular elements are too nearly alike in size and are too statically placed in the layout area for effective display. At the right a more dramatic use of circular elements creates rhythmic progression by placement and variation of size and tone.

At bottom right, the left example suffers by the mechanical division of space and the ponderous solid at bottom, whose rectangularity emphasizes its blatancy.

The central layout interestingly divides the space with the vertical initial and the lighter-toned horizontal band at the bottom. The italic "deas" gives a certain momentum to the lettering. The last sketch shows how a solid brush stroke type of panel at the top may be enhanced by a lighter toned over-all tint background that bleeds at all edges.

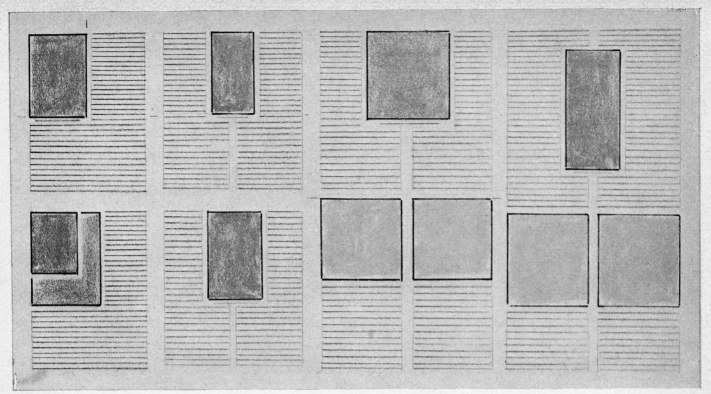

First column top—A pictorial element incorrectly divides a text mass mathematically in half, both vertically and horizontally. In the example beneath it a more interesting layout is attained by reduction or enlargement of the pictorial element to avoid a mathematical division of text area.

Second column top—The pictorial element divides a page of text into three mathematically alike areas across two columns and in half from top to bottom. The lower sketch enlarges the pictorial element so that the eye does not readily perceive mathematical relationship.

Third arrangement—Three mathematically alike pictorial elements are monotonously placed in two columns of text while in the fourth arrangement the pictorial elements are lengthened vertically and placed more interestingly to achieve a better divisioning and allocation of text areas.

THE THREE PANELS on the opposite page contain basic diagrammatic sketches which illustrate the subtle influences that size, shape, tone and position of elements exert on the pattern of a layout. These elements are purposely drawn in a vague style to symbolize masses and units as they may be interpreted in line or halftone plates, reverse and screen tint areas, type lines and masses, rules, panels, borders, logotypes and other elements.

CONTRAST—*Top left panel*

The top three examples illustrate how contrast in direction may be achieved by placing horizontal, vertical, circular, diagonal and irregularly shaped elements so that the movement of the eye is influenced by the directional shape of the element. The first example illustrates the natural movement of the eye to the right caused by a horizontal shape, then the downward vertical movement, into the circular form, thence to the left horizontal lines. In the second example the top semi-circular form is a focal point from which the eye gravitates downward vertically, then to the right and into the irregular element at extreme bottom right.

The third example follows naturally from left to right, then diagonally downward to lower left, and horizontally to the right.

The remaining examples in this panel show further how directional contrast is emphasized.

RHYTHM—*Top right panel*

The top left example emphasizes the function of contrasting shapes and the introduction of a rhythmic touch that connects the top and bottom elements with its graceful sweep.

Rhythm in the top right example is emphasized by the swift directional movement of the arrow placed in accentuation to the rectangular horizontal and vertical elements. It carries the eye emphatically to the text at extreme right.

In the other examples, extreme shapes are used to illustrate the emphatic movement exerted by these elements. Movement emanates from a circular form more smoothly than from an element that has sharply accentuated features, such as the points of a star. Likewise, diagonals create more movement than horizontal and vertical shapes.

Repetition of similarly shaped elements, such as the circular forms in the lower left example, or the horizontal display elements in the lower right, creates rhythm when they are placed in an orderly, logical pattern for the eye to follow.

UNITY—*Panel across bottom*

The basic fundamental for attaining unity is the grouping together of all related elements, thus reducing the number of display elements and simplifying the pattern.

All the elemental examples in the bottom panel are themselves unified by placement together.

The examples at extreme left show how related elements may be grouped by means of borders, background panels and overlapping of elements.

The examples at the right illustrate how unity may be achieved by a simple device such as a rule, initial letter, border or bracket, which may be used as an axis or focal point for grouping type masses and other elements.

Democracy in Action is Beating Moscow in Western Europe

Collier's correspondent sees surprising resurgence of non-Communist strength and spirit—even in Berlin

THERE'S a new battle cry of freedom sounding out in increasing volume from millions and millions of throats in war-wracked Europe.

Over here we hear it only faintly as yet — hard to distinguish above the clamor and din of Communist bombast.

But Quentin Reynolds has heard this modern, spirited singing of the old battle cry in the Western European countries—heard it growing in power, in volume, in confidence even in Berlin.

Collier's sent this war-seasoned correspondent back to Europe on a fact hunt. Were the Soviets winning the cold war? Was the spirit of democracy, as we know it, dead? Was the news all bad?

Reynolds finds hope in the ruin and rubble. He finds massed millions roaring approval of democracy in open defiance of Soviet edicts. He finds the spirit of democracy stronger, more active, more militant than ever before. Reynolds writes:

"A year ago, anyone who suggested that there were Germans willing to shed their blood for democratic ideals would have been greeted with cynical laughter   Today German blood *has* been shed in defense of democracy.

This almost unbelievable resurgence of the democratic spirit is not confined to Germany. It is gathering strength all over Europe, and wherever it gains there is a corresponding weakening of Communism."

Read *Europe's Battle Cry of Freedom* by Quentin Reynolds in Collier's, out today, for a heartening close-up of reawakened and revitalized peoples waging a winning fight against Communism.

The World's Fastest Letter Carrier

Imagine sending a four-page love letter in your own handwriting to your girl three thousand miles away, and getting a four-page answer while you wait! The scientific miracle that will make this possible goes by the unromantic name of Ultrafax. It transmits messages, maps, pictures at the speed of the television eye — sends "Gone with the Wind" in 90 seconds. How does it work? Read A MILLION WORDS A MINUTE, the fascinating story of an invention that is sure to revolutionize communication.

Is This The Key To Lower Food Bills?

The key to lower food bills is *really* a key — in Memphis. For Clarence Saunders, inventor of Piggly Wiggly has done it again with Keedoozle, a store in which a key substitutes for clerks. It works something like a dial telephone, with groceries taking the place of numbers and a camera-like key replacing the dial. Anyway, Saunders manages to sell packaged groceries faster and cheaper, and all Memphis is raving, and saving. See FROM PIGGLY WIGGLY TO KEEDOOZLE.

If you haven't read Collier's lately, there's a parade of surprises in store for you. Get it today and see.

Are You Driving Your Husband To Failure?

Are you help or hindrance to your husband's career? Don't be too quick to answer that. According to an eminent psychoanalyst, many wives who think they're spurring their spouses to greater effort, actually drive them to drink, or inferiority complexes. Read HOW TO DEVOUR YOUR HUSBAND, and decide how you rate as a helpmeet.

Plus such top fiction as Collier's Star Story, YOU CAN GET JUST SO MUCH JUSTICE — a spine-tingling tale of murder and a witness whose lips were sealed by fear. And comics, features — a whole big book of great reading.

More than ever *

the BUY is

Collier's
THE NATIONAL WEEKLY

* New in cover, in layout, in typography, Collier's, more than ever, is the buy for advertisers who expect a dollar to do 100 cents' worth of work. For Collier's millions of families are — *Young* enough to need things. *Active* enough to want things. *Prosperous* enough to buy things. And Collier's cost per page is still low enough to permit adequate frequency of insertion.

The Crowell-Collier Publishing Company, 250 Park Avenue, New York 17, N. Y. — Publishers of Collier's, The American Magazine, Woman's Home Companion

The Collier's ad above is reduced about one half actual size, primarily to illustrate *unity*. Note how the three small illustrated panels at bottom left are unified with the Collier's logotype and other smaller elements by means of rules. Heading, illustration and text are likewise effectively allocated to achieve a well-balanced, unified layout. Type is Bodoni with proper lettering accompaniment.

The Newsweek ad at the right is also reduced half original newspaper size. It likewise typifies *unity* of pattern, in a more dominant structure. Note that the unifying element that joins the top and bottom of layout is the "product" itself. The main heading is hand lettered. Headings for the small blocks of Bookman type are Spartan and Beton Extra Bold. The "blurbs" at bottom left are hand lettered.

COMING EVENTS!

HOW LONG CAN OUR AIR FORCE KEEP THE PEACE?

Do we know our own strength? Could we stop Russia today? Who can better answer these questions than General Carl Spaatz, retired head of the U. S. Air Force? And he does answer them—in his column of opinion on MILITARY AFFAIRS in the current Newsweek. It's an expert's opinion respected from Washington to Moscow. It's an opinion every American should read. It's in the new Newsweek, out on all newsstands today.

WILL BUMPER CROPS MEAN LOWER PRICES?

Record grain and cotton crops are reported. Will they really mean lower food and clothing prices? Can your budget expect relief? You'll find the facts about future prices—facts that affect your pocketbook—in the WASHINGTON TRENDS section of the new Newsweek—now on all newsstands.

HOW LONG CAN WE COUNT ON MIDDLE EAST OIL?

We're importing Middle East oil now. Our plans for the recovery of Western Europe depend on it, too. And its importance will be magnified many times in the event of war. So Middle East oil is of vital interest to every American. You'll want to read what Newsweek expert Ernest K. Lindley has to say about it in his signed column of opinion, WASHINGTON TIDES. Read it in the current issue of Newsweek.

WILL THE ARABS QUIT IN ISRAEL?

The turmoil in Israel is about to reach a climax. What will it be? How will it all end? Readers of the current Newsweek will get a preview. For Newsweek's PERISCOPE takes a long, searching look and comes up with a prediction. You'll want to be in on it. Look in the PERISCOPE section of the new Newsweek.

How Newsweek Keeps You Ahead of the Headlines

It happens too often to be called luck . too consistently for coincidence. For instance, Newsweek's Periscope forecast the Berlin crisis six weeks before it happened. Russia's Czechoslovakian coup nine months ahead of the headlines.

No, this matter of Newsweek calling the turn can be marked up to just one thing. The ability to interpret a news story like a road map . where it began . . . where it is today . . . where it will be tomorrow. And to do it, Newsweek calls on a world-wide staff of experts . . . on a team of news analysts unmatched by any other magazine. Analysts and experts who weigh the facts without prejudice, draw objective conclusions.

The signed opinions of experts like Henry Hazlitt in Business, General Spaatz on Military Affairs, Ernest K. Lindley in National Affairs, Raymond Moley in Politics, Joseph B. Phillips in Foreign Affairs . these are the men who give Newsweek readers something no other magazine supplies. A crystal-clear picture of what's happened .. why it's happened and what's going to happen next.

To Newsweek readers this view of the future is *vitally important*. So these 770,000 alert, far-sighted American families who must make tomorrow's decisions today, read Newsweek from cover to cover every week. To them Newsweek is "must" reading—for it keeps them ahead of the headlines.

SEPTEMBER 20, 1948

Newsweek
THE MAGAZINE OF NEWS SIGNIFICANCE

20c

FROM THE AD MAN'S POINT OF VIEW, NEWSWEEK IS BETTER THAN EVER. DID YOU SEE THEIR NEW SURVEY?

I SURE DID AND SOME OF THE NUMBERS ARE STARTLING. BETTER THAN 4 OUT OF 5 NEWSWEEK READERS ARE LEADERS IN BUSINESS INDUSTRY AND THE PROFESSIONS . . . BY FAR THE GREATEST CONCENTRATION OF ANY GENERAL MAGAZINE . . . AT THE LOWEST COST PER THOUSAND. I'LL SAY NEWSWEEK IS BETTER THAN EVER!

The average annual income of Newsweek families puts them in the top 4% of the nation

The Magazine of News Significance

On sale today 20¢

Facing Page Layouts

IN PLANNING the facing pages of a pictorial broadside, booklet, house organ or magazine, where the prime objective is to present the picture story in a predominating manner with limited textual elements, it is obvious that the more unrestrained the pattern of the spread appears, the more effective and dramatic will be the presentation.

The most important basic technique for "bridging the gutter" is to create an optical continuity which carries one's vision across the central vertical fold in a subtle, effortless manner. When the facing pages comprise the center spread, the composition is more readily attained and the mechanics simplified, but even when the pages are separately printed to fold and bind together as a spread they should be so designed that the desired pattern is achieved regardless.

Bleeding pictorial elements off the pages of spreads at various points helps to create the feeling of expansiveness, but care must be taken not to overdo bleeds. One relieves the monotony of too many bleed pictures by surrounding them with white space of the proper proportions and placing them interestingly in relation to other horizontal, vertical or circular shapes.

Having attained a basic allocation of all pictorial elements in a thumbnail by careful attention to proper proportioning of all elements and their placement to avoid mathematical relationship, the next most important step is their unification so that the eye encompasses the double-spread as a unit.

It bears repetition here that layout serves its purpose well if the mechanics of reproduction are foremost in the mind of the layout man as he evolves the basic thumbnails. As the planning progresses, every application of design should be predicated on its helpfulness to the reproductive method rather than the achievement of some artistic whim or fancy.

Whether the reproduction is by letterpress, offset or gravure, certain basic procedures and techniques are equally applicable. For example, it is inadvisable to position certain forms of typographical headings across the "gutter," or binding edge, in such a manner as to preclude the possibility of proper alignment, tone or color matching, word and letter spacing. It is equally inadvisable to place certain types of illustrative elements in positions that endanger their proper negative splitting and, through unanticipated irregularities in folding and binding, decrease the effectiveness of the ultimate printing.

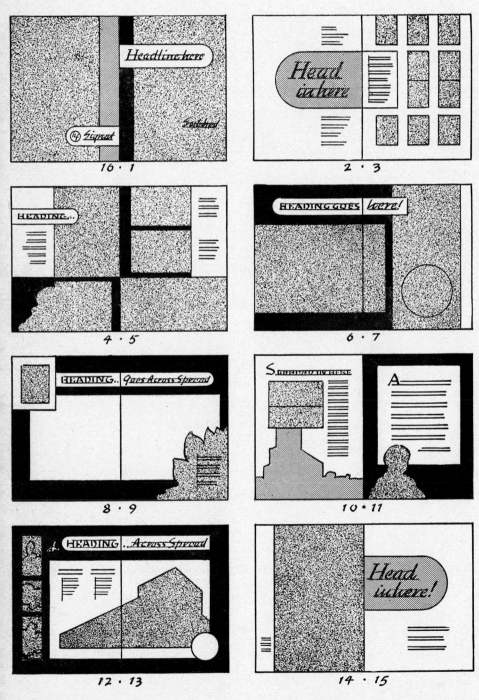

The thumbnails above are for a typical 16-page, self-cover, vertical pictorial booklet. The thumbnails present broad patterns representing illustrative or typographic elements of a variable nature which can be changed to meet the needs of specific material.

The sketches basically illustrate the princi-

ple of applying *unity* by placement, grouping and the proper allocation of white space.

The top left thumbnail illustrates the allocation of elements on the first and last page of the booklet. Here a single horizontal solid band is used to tie in the heading on Page 1 with the pictorial element which bleeds top, bottom and right side. The contrasting tonal vertical gives added emphasis and depth. On page 16 the signature and logotype are placed logically at the bottom right in a signing-off position, reiterating the principle that natural optical progression is from top left to bottom right.

The horizontal panel on the layout to the right, running from Page 2 into the well-unified group of black pictorial elements on Page 3 cohesively "bridges the gutter" and optically unifies all elements. Pages 4 and 5 are unified by vertical and horizontal elements which terminate at the binding edge of both left and right-hand pages. Comfortable white margins at left and right sides of the spread on which the captions are positioned aid unification process.

The broad horizontal black element running from Page 6 onto Page 7 as well as the head-band at top, requires splitting of both negatives in photo-mechanical reproduction. The heading likewise requires the proper breaking of copy for correct positioning of type on either side of the gutter. The width of the head-band obviously is predicated on the copy.

Pages 8 and 9 are effectively unified with an over-all background pattern whose broad expanse accents the display importance of such a spread.

Pages 10 and 11 are effectively unified by a tonal pattern across both pages which is effectively mortised on the right page to emphasize the lower silhouetted figure.

Pages 12 and 13 use the heading technique of 6 and 7 in reverse and the mortise in another effective manner.

Pages 14 and 15 "echo" the pattern of pages 2 and 3 with a large closing illustration at the left.

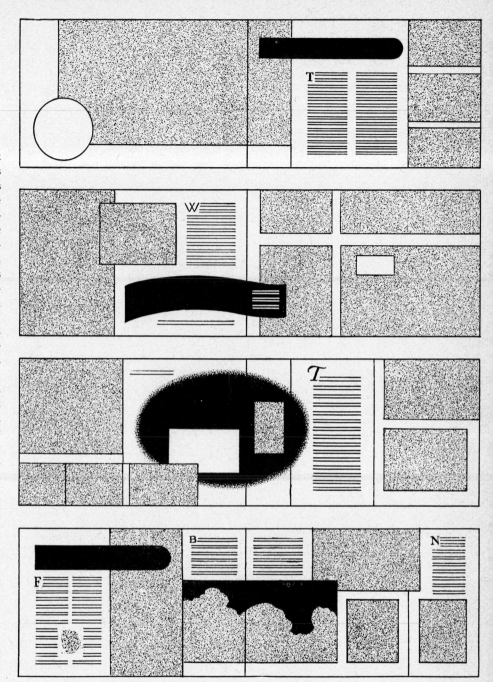

The large horizontal pictorial element which dominates the top spread at right has prime attention value. Its shape promotes directional movement to the right across the gutter, which is accentuated by the horizontal solid band at the top. While the individual shapes of the three right illustrations also accentuate directional movement, the grouping of the three unified elements is definitely vertical, to add directional contrast and interest, as do the two vertical columns of text.

The circular element, bottom left, pleasantly relieves the monotony of too many angular shapes, as does the circular extremity of the top right solid band.

Throughout these thumbnails, lettered suggestions for definite use of many predominating elements is omitted so that the pattern may be applicable to variations of textual copy, type styles, tonal qualities of halftones, etc. For example, the circular element at bottom left could enclose a line illustration, wash drawing or a subordinate block of text. The solid head-band could have a line of type on it in reverse. Ample space is available beneath the dominating illustration for a caption or additional text. In the second spread, the dominating solid band sweeps dynamically across the gutter to unify the large right grouping of pictorial elements with the left of the page. Here five elements bleed off the edges to amplify the expansiveness of the pictures while the one in top center at the left is accentuated with white space at three sides. The text column and the extreme left vertical illustration, contrast the horizontal movement, as does the vertical element at bottom left of the right page. Note that while the dominant band sweeps directly across the gutter, a suggestion is made that short text copy may be reversed at the extreme right division while the dominant heading copy could be surprinted on the left pattern.

In the third spread a wider variety of pictorial shapes is suggested. The four ele-

ments at the left are unified by grouping together and overlapping the fourth on the dominating solid whose oval-shape spreads across the gutter and acts as a background for two other rectangular elements. The vertical column of type and white space surrounding it emphasizes the text.

Broader allocation is given text blocks in the last example, which employs a different treatment entirely across the gutter.

Here the silhouetted contour of the central illustration is accentuated by the horizontal solid background upon which a heading or subheading could be surprinted or reversed to amplify the heading or illustrative element that may be placed on the dominantly solid band at top left. The interesting pattern of white space created by the placement of all elements, by its irregularity relieves the entire pattern.

Allotment of White Space PART FIVE

WHITE SPACE is the medium through which relief and freedom are imparted to a layout; through which it gets interesting "breathing space," and without which overcrowding and stiltedness might prevail. White space, when correctly applied, prevents monotony, helps direct attention, contrasts or emphasizes elements, and assists in stimulating optical rhythm.

The influence that white space exerts on a layout may be likened to the introduction of open spaces for sunlight, ventilation and recreational areas in the plan of a community.

The layout expert, by experience, will have acquired a subconscious sense of space division and allocation, and this influences him as he shapes and places the units and masses. The student, however, should pause often as a layout progresses to make a detailed check of all white space to evaluate its effectiveness.

At this point it is well to explain the advantages of working with tracing tissue. Having ascertained that some of the units in a fairly completed layout seem crowded, or the white areas incorrectly proportioned or allocated, the layout can be placed under another tissue on which the dimensions of the layout area have been ruled. The original layout can then be moved about, new patterns evaluated on the top sheet and refinements made to secure better distribution of white space.

Minor cropping or changing of contours of certain illustrations, slight enlargement, reduction or reshaping of type masses, re-arranging of display lines or shifting of certain elements may often improve the effectiveness of white space.

One should be careful, however, not to deviate materially from the original basic design, to destroy any of the subtle creative qualities that may already have been achieved, or to impair proportion and balance of the units. If improvement is not readily attained without undue distortion of elements, it may be advisable to discard the entire layout and revert to making a new thumbnail.

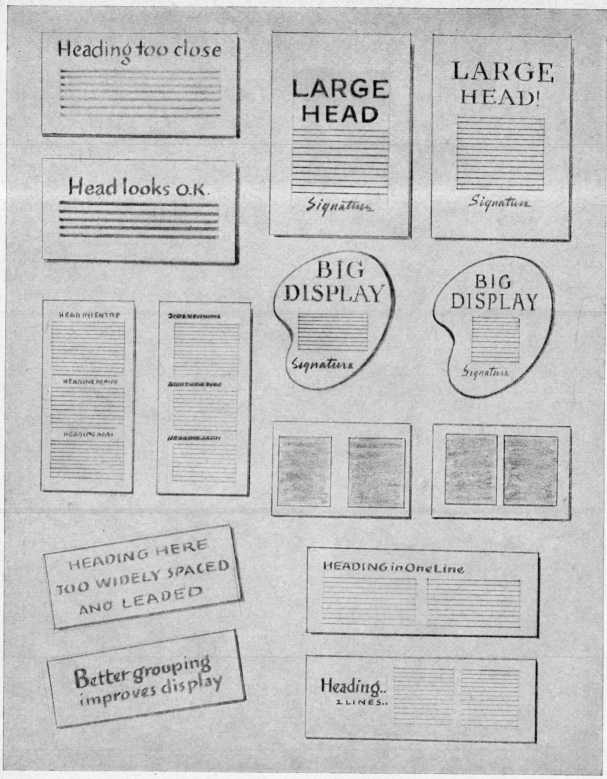

Seven pairs of analytical pencil roughs showing improved use of white space in the redrawn version of each initial attempt. In the first revision, the heading is pulled away from the top edge, equalizing margins and improving display value. In the pair to the right, improvement in balance is shown by the transposition of space to the bottom margin. The left center pair shows how the monotony of centered heads and equal side margins can be eliminated by placing subheads at side and indenting the text masses more at the left. The units in the first rough "Big Display" crowd the area too much. Better emphasis is given smaller elements by more white space. The pair directly beneath show how two widely separated elements, placed too low in an area, can be unified and properly placed by redistribution of space to side margins and to the bottom. These units may be visualized as two facing text pages, or illustrations that are related. The lettering in the bottom left pair is self-explanatory. The last pair shows a more informal re-setting that directs attention to the heading and activates the composition by lavish use of white space.

Every layout has many potentialities for correct space division and distribution. One should not be dismayed if the copy seems inconsistent with the layout area. There is always some graphic method by which an interesting design may be accomplished.

Where copy is limited and space plentiful, the layout area may be divided subtly into smaller areas by the ingenious use of rules, ornamentation, type lines, screen tint patterns, reverse panels, initial letters and other elements—and the various units interestingly shaped and positioned within these smaller areas.

Obviously, where copy and illustrations are plentiful and space is limited, all elements should be reduced to their minimum—unimportant units subordinated, related units and masses combined, and all positioned in the layout area to achieve the most effective allocation of white space.

In the text masses of a composition there are many seemingly inconsequential elements that exert great influence on the structural qualities and tone of a layout. They are the spaces between letters, words, paragraphs and lines of type; likewise paragraph indentations, spaces between type and rules, type captions and cuts and between columns of text matter. These should always be carefully regulated and instructions precisely designated on the copy and layout for the guidance of the typographer.

No element of white space should be considered too unimportant to receive proper attention. Even when the layout has been processed by the typographer, minor corrections in spacing ofttimes may be made on the type proofs to make the finished product more effective.

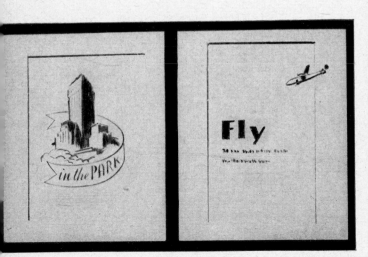 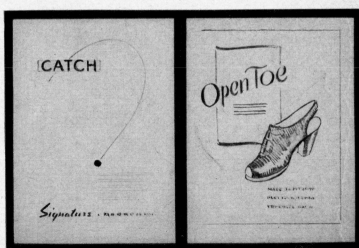

The roughs in these panels illustrate how white space contrasts and accentuates.

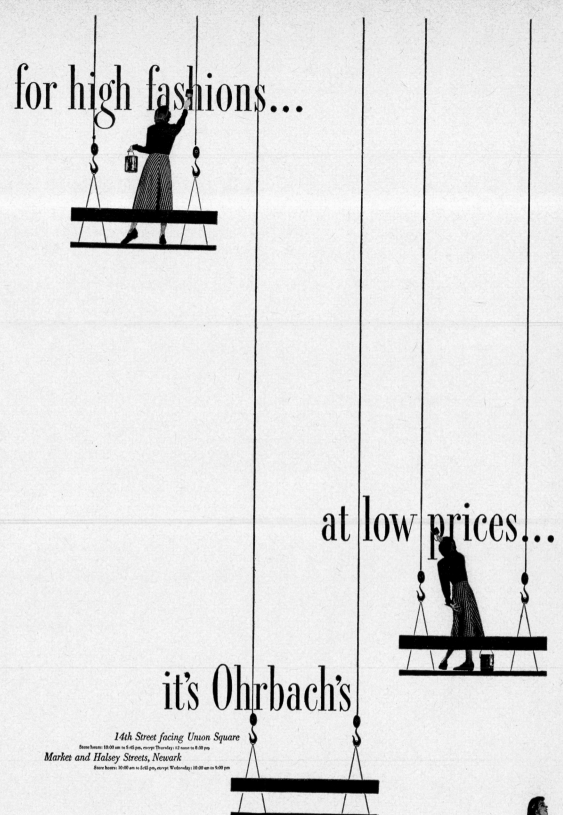

for high fashions...

at low prices...

it's Ohrbach's

14th Street facing Union Square
Store hours: 10:00 am to 5:45 pm, except Thursday: 12 noon to 8:30 pm
Market and Halsey Streets, Newark
Store hours: 10:00 am to 5:45 pm, except Wednesday: 10:00 am to 9:00 pm

Reproduction of a full-page informally balanced
newspaper advertisement which illustrates how
lavish white space may effectively be allocated to
direct attention. Note the slender, graceful lettering for the three display lines which accentuates
the vertical patterns. The type is Bodoni Book.

"A business in millions...a profit in pennies"

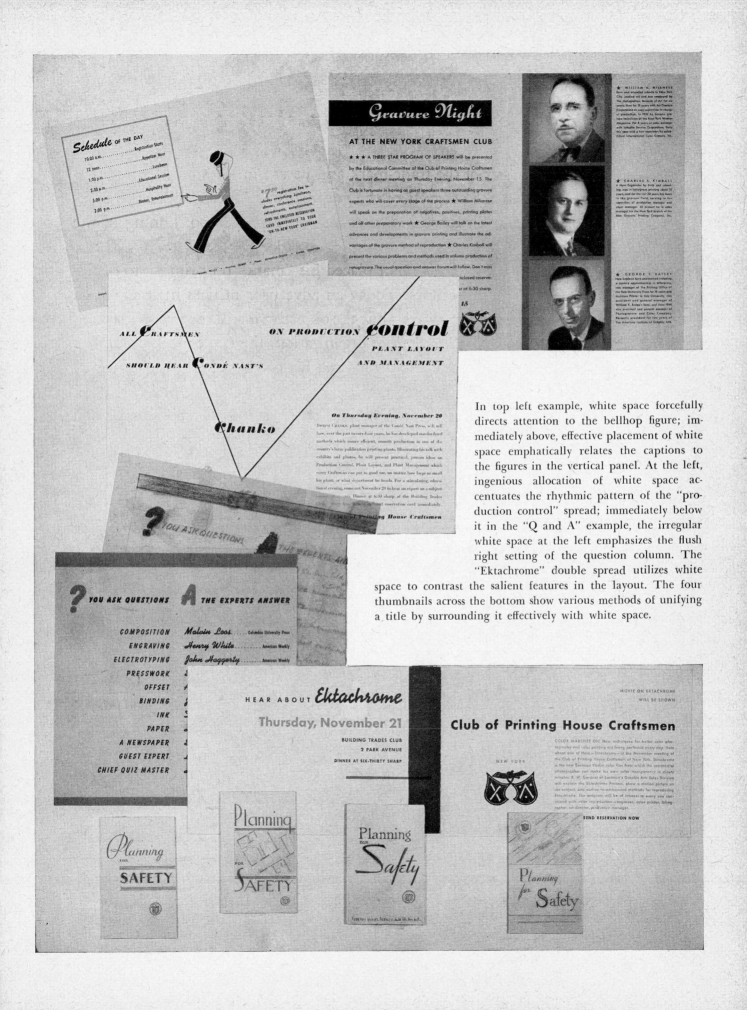

In top left example, white space forcefully directs attention to the bellhop figure; immediately above, effective placement of white space emphatically relates the captions to the figures in the vertical panel. At the left, ingenious allocation of white space accentuates the rhythmic pattern of the "production control" spread; immediately below it in the "Q and A" example, the irregular white space at the left emphasizes the flush right setting of the question column. The "Ektachrome" double spread utilizes white space to contrast the salient features in the layout. The four thumbnails across the bottom show various methods of unifying a title by surrounding it effectively with white space.

Positioning the Trade-mark

THE DEVELOPMENT of the trade-mark and its use in layout is a most interesting chapter in the progress of the graphic arts. A brief evaluation of its purpose will assist in formulating methods for proper positioning of the trade-mark.

In the early days, a craftsman placed his "mark" on printing to distinguish it from his competitors. Today an advertiser utilizes his trade-mark in many more diversified ways—but the objective is still the same. Through constant association with a firm or organization, the trade-mark becomes a symbol of individuality for its owner and his product.

In determining the proper position for the trade-mark, the elemental factors to be considered are the ultimate objective of the copy theme and the relative importance of the trade-mark in the layout pattern.

Obviously, if an advertisement is of an institutional nature, which aims to publicize the trade-mark primarily, it should be placed in the most conspicuous position to dominate the layout. When the purpose is to accentuate some quality or function of the product itself, the trade-mark must accordingly be placed in a less conspicuous position; its size, tone value and position subtly subordinated in the design.

Positioning of the trade-mark should be done adroitly, with proper regard for the size, shape and tone values of both the display units and the trade-mark itself.

The trade-mark should be studied carefully and then so positioned that it accentuates the design qualities of its elements. Trade-marks having design qualities that are formally balanced may be placed in reposeful positions. The details of others suggest motion in a particular direction and the position of these trade-marks, obviously, should be in accord with their design elements. Likewise, the movement in pictures or other display elements should be studied so that in grouping them with a trade-mark, visual direction is properly coordinated.

Positioning a trade-mark so that it will subtly combine two harmonious

What is a Shirt? Just buttons, thread, fabric?

Our shirts, made meticulously to your measure, start at $4.95

when three or more are ordered.

The Custom Shop
Shirtmakers

In New York City. 245 Park Ave. 37 West 48th St. 38 East 43rd St. 555 Lexington Ave. 283 Madison Ave.
1370 Broadway. 1 Rector St. 55 Liberty St. Other stores: Brooklyn, Newark, Philadelphia, Washington.

The Custom Shop
Shirtmakers

In New York
245 Park Avenue
37 West 48th Street
38 East 43rd Street
555 Lexington Avenue
283 Madison Avenue
1370 Broadway
55 Liberty Street
1 Rector Street
Other stores
Brooklyn
Newark
Philadelphia
Washington

shirts   made-to-measure

Meticulously tailored.
When three or more
are ordered
. . from **$4.95**

In New York: 245 Park Ave. 37 West 48th St. 38 East 43rd St. 555 Lexington Ave. 283 Madison Ave.
1370 Broadway. 1 Rector St. 55 Liberty St. Other stores: Brooklyn, Newark, Philadelphia, Washington

The Custom Shop
Shirtmakers

We'll cut your favorite collar
or design one specially for you
and make your shirt to measure. Prices begin at $4.95
when three or more shirts are ordered.

Three variations of logotype placement, from a
series that employs white space advantageously.

Individualized trade-marks and logotypes, as used by consistent
advertisers to distinguish and individualize their advertising, are
shown above in a cross-section of metropolitan New York advertising.

The "Provident" emblem combines with the
Company name to give this formal arrangement a heading of character.

Peck and Peck

Peck and
Peck

At extreme left are two variations of a finely hand-lettered
logotype while at left is the
Christmas version of the logo created for holiday advertising only.

display elements obviates the trade-mark being loosely placed. This further assists in reducing the number of design elements and helps achieve unity.

Placing a trade-mark alone in a large area of white space gives it more attention value than if it is placed close to type masses or illustrations. Care should be taken, however, to keep its size dignified and proportionate to other elements in the composition.

Where color is employed in printing, it often enhances effectiveness of the trade-mark. The symbol itself, some interesting or forceful part thereof, or its surrounding area or embellishment may be accentuated with color, according to the emphasis desired.

Due to the varied uses required of a trade-mark, it is essential that it be of sound design and simple artistic expressiveness.

Many trade-marks of ancient heritage are constantly being refined artistically to meet the needs of modern creative and reproductive processes. Basic designs are retained while contours and other features are revamped to conform to improved layout techniques. Many old trade-marks, however, which are still being used in their original form often tax the ingenuity of the layout man.

Such an outmoded trade-mark requires subtle treatment. Toning its weight with a halftone screen, placing it on a screen tint background, reversing it on a solid or screened background, surrounding it with properly associated type or subordinating it pictorially, can often bring an outmoded trade-mark into better relationship with the art work, typography and general theme of the layout.

The Logotype

A logotype is an unusual lettered or typographical interpretation of a name, slogan, service or product, which is used as an individual display symbol, the purpose and functions of which are somewhat similar to those of the trade-mark.

The logotype can be used in conjunction with a trade-mark, widely separated in the layout or combined with the trade-mark to form one unit.

While the trade-mark must always retain its fundamental design, styles

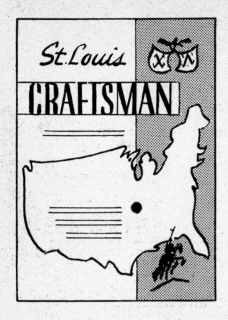

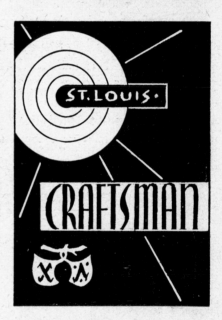

Nine idea sketches for a bulletin cover, each of which evaluates the
placement of the Craftsman Club emblem in a different manner.

and treatments of logotypes may vary with the style and pattern of the layout. The variety in design and application of logotypes is limited only by the ingenuity of the layout man and the spontaneity which the layout process develops.

Logotypes of simple design may be incorporated in display lines, text masses or used as signatures. Those of more ornate design must be used sparingly. Their design features should be critically analyzed and their tone and position in a layout regulated accordingly.

The value of a trade-mark or logotype is increased tremendously if its style is readily adaptable to the many varied formats and different methods of reproduction. Should the layout man have any part in creating a trade-mark or logotype, he should regulate its design, contours and reproductive qualities to serve this purpose.

Collecting distinctive and unusual trade-marks and logotypes from magazines and newspapers will aid materially in evaluating the unlimited possibilities for placing trade-marks and logotypes.

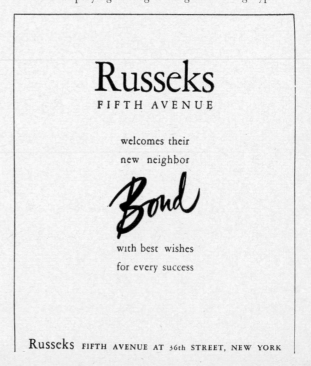

Left—Eight thumbnails which evaluate the size and position of the "kf" logotype differently.

Below—A large metropolitan space user devotes some of it to displaying a neighboring store's logotype.

Ornamentation

ORNAMENTATION, when applied correctly, relieves monotony and adds touches of charm and relief to a composition which otherwise might appear rigid and severe.

Ornamentation has gone through many phases of development since the flowery era of Gutenberg but its fundamental purpose prevails. The lacy trimmings, curlicues and shaded rules of yesterday have been replaced with a more simple decorativeness that better fits the modern tempo.

True, certain modern treatments are not always applicable to every layout style, but perusal of the pages of leading periodicals will prove that the current trend toward simplicity and restraint in ornamentation is worthy of emulation.

There are but few fundamental rules to guide one in achieving correct ornamentation. Continued experiments and practice will do most to develop in one the ability to sense when a layout needs decoration, the good taste to choose the proper ornamentation, and the ability to limit its application to the required minimum.

Restraint in ornamentation is of prime importance. A fault which is common with the beginner is that of overemphasis in decoration and the desire to fill all available white space with ornamentation.

A composition that is embellished with an overabundance of rules, borders, ornaments or other freakish decoration calls attention primarily to the ornamental qualities and subordinates the message.

Ornamentation should be unobtrusive. It should be subtly felt, rather than blatantly seen. The tone value of ornamentation must be harmonious with the display units and typography. In general, no detail of the ornamenting element, be it a type ornament, rule, border or background pattern, should have greater display value than the display units or masses which it adorns. Neither should its values be, by comparison, weak or inharmonious.

101

As a simple illustration, a rectangular border around several display lines may be relatively weak and ineffective or blatant and overemphasized, according to the weight of the border. Likewise, a screen tint background for type or lettering can be an effective contrasting element or it can be a detracting feature, according to its tone value.

The techniques, tonal values and distinguishing characteristics of art work, lettering, halftones and accompanying typography, should also govern the selection of ornamentation. For example, a layout containing a colonial-type illustration, delicate Caslon type, swash initials and other elements of similar character requires decorative ornamentation to accentuate the old-style pattern.

A layout containing broad bleed illustrations, reverse panels, bold sans-serif types and other elements exemplifying the modern trend, obviously requires a treatment that emphasizes the strength and simplicity of that style. Every layout, therefore, should be thoroughly evaluated to ascertain the proper style, tone and other accentuating characteristics required of its ornamentation.

Above are typical examples of the style of layout prevalent in the 1920s interpreted with the traditional typography and harmonizing pictorial elements and ornamentation.

Examples of contemporary design which utilizes a more dynamic typography accentuated by a more simplified ornamentation and pictorial accompaniment.

Type founders' specimen sheets are excellent for reference in choosing the proper style of ornamentation for a particular type. The sketches below were made by first tracing the type lines and then experimenting with the accompanying decorative devices for proper accentuation.

Experimental sketches showing initial letters, decorative borders and lettering subtly ornamented with appropriate illustrative symbols. This type of ornamentation requires hand lettering and cuts—a cost factor to consider.

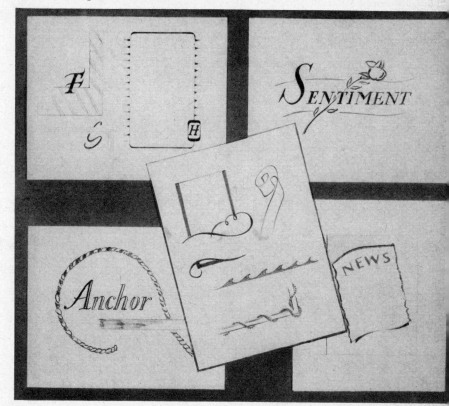

Where color is applied for ornamentation, particular care must be taken to coordinate its color value with the tone of all other elements. Decoration that may appear harmonious in black will appear weak and ineffective if printed in pastel or light colors. Similarly, backgrounds that may be correct in light colors will overshadow type that overprints them if they are printed in deep shades of color.

Initial letters, rules and decorations that are to print in color should be specified in a proportionately heavier weight than the remainder of the layout that is to print in black.

Practicability in mechanical reproduction should govern typographical ornamentation. There is available in the modern composing room an almost unlimited variety of rules, ornaments, dingbats, and other typographical decorators, which together with screen tint patterns, reverse plates and other photoengraving processes may be employed to achieve effective ornamentation with a minimum of art work.

Reverse Backgrounds
Toned Areas

REVERSE BACKGROUNDS and toned areas have many diversified design and ornamental functions in modern layout techniques. The fundamental objective behind their use is the creation of emphatic tonal contrasts and gradations which add interest and sparkle to a composition.

An almost unlimited variety of tones and patterns is possible through the utilization of the many types of positive plates and screen tints available in photoengraving, gravure and offset.

The "positive" plate is one in which type, lettering or a line illustration appears in white on a solid black or screened background.

Halftone screen tints of many shades may be used as background patterns for type, lettering, ornamentation or line illustrations in black or white; as borders, panels and as toning mediums for type and line illustrations. Positives and screen tints of varying tones, likewise, may be combined to form a variety of interesting patterns. The principle that limited gray tones added to black and white makes for more interesting contrast is the basis for using these combinations.

Effective patterns are achieved by ingenious control of shapes and tone values in positive plates and screen tints and their proper combination with type, rules, pictures and other elements.

Restraint is to be advocated in specifying large black areas, both for design and reproductive reasons. The eye will absorb large areas of gray more comfortably than expansive black masses which ofttimes create a funereal atmosphere.

Large black areas may also create undue makeready and presswork problems which may be obviated by utilizing screen tints. Large solid areas or positive plates printed in proper colors, however, add interest and attention value.

104

The same fundamental principles which govern the placement of type and other elements in a specified area should be used in positioning elements in a positive plate or screen tint background. Correct positioning, with proper margins, is most essential in preparing reproduction copy for photoengraving because the finished engravings cannot be altered.

Generally, script or other delicate type with fine lines and serifs should be avoided in positive plates.

Before definitely deciding values for reverse backgrounds and toned areas evaluation may be made with black and gray paper of various shades which conform to the tonal values of tints available in photoengraving, offset or gravure. The various elements can be trimmed to size, pasted down and sketched thereon to evaluate different techniques.

Reverse and toned areas may be designated on roughs by sketching on both sides of the tissue. For example, black or dark gray elements may be drawn on the front, while the lighter gray areas may be drawn on the reverse side with varying shades of pencil, gray crayon or water color. Proper screen line values should be specified to the engraver, and a sample of the paper stock to be used should be submitted for proofing of cuts. When in doubt his advice should be highly regarded, as the effective interpretation of reverse backgrounds and toned areas, as drawn on the layout, depends upon attaining correct photoengraving values in the finished plates.

The modern-type layout with its simplicity of line and movement employs the various engraving patterns extensively for decorative purposes. This seems an appropriate place to familiarize the layout student with some of the technical terms for specifying copy to be engraved.

Screen tint patterns may be designated on the reverse of layout tissue with a broad flat pencil. The similarity of tone in the layout to the specified screen can be fairly well regulated by controlling the pressure and amount of graphite.

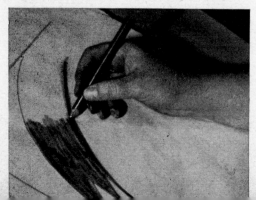

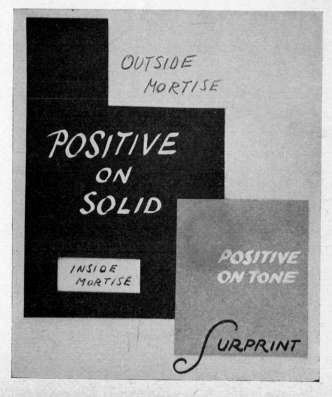

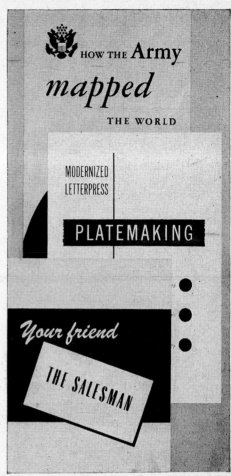

The "A-B-C's" grouping at the top, left, shows: the two-color rough on which all typographical specifications are clearly defined; below it a proof of the composing room interpretation (note the comic figure composed of parentheses, rules and dingbats); a proof of the complete form with "positive" plate of central area in position. The job is now ready for electrotyping, duplicate plates and routing for color separation.

At top right in vertical sequence are shown: surprints of three lines of well-emphasized Garamond Bold type on a screen tint background; News Gothic Condensed type reversed on a horizontal hand drawn panel; a line of Brush, "Your friend," combined with an angular setting of "The Salesman," in Radiant Bold Condensed in a rule shadow box was sufficient copy for the engraving of the two-color reproduction.

Across the bottom are: the explicitly marked rough which guided all mechanical procedures of "First-Hand Facts on Fotosetter," the black and white drawing with type cemented in position, and the direct mail piece produced therefrom.

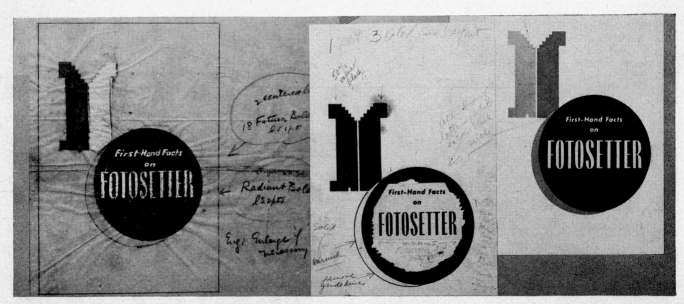

Right—In the first example, a capital "S" is reversed on a vertically shaped color block of sufficient size to accentuate the initial, yet small enough to permit placement of the remaining lower case letters of the word "style" in fairly close proximity so that the continuity of reading is not upset. The top right layout forcefully displays the main heading in reverse with a screen tint as a background panel on which a decorative motif has been reversed. The lower right corner may be utilized for additional copy. The "Punch" thumbnail at upper left reverses the catchline on a brush-stroked, solid element placed at left top dominating position. Its slanting directional quality gives momentum to the element which is counterbalanced by the placid tonal background which offers a spacious pattern for surprinting.

Immediately beneath is another variation of the slanted pattern theme. Limited use of slanted elements is advocated on the basis that an occasional relief to the eye is welcome when most elements are rectangular but that if many elements are non-rectangular too much action defeats the main purpose, which is to achieve contrast.

The small vertical pattern in the center of the group gives dominant "positive" emphasis to the large initial "T" alongside of which a variety of display or text lines may be placed. The circular element maintains optical balance at the lower right and the white space at the bottom invitingly suggests relatively less important text and signature elements. The right central thumbnail reverses a lower case "d" on a solid background in such a size and manner as to have the "waistline" portion of the initial form an interesting enclosure for the text mass shown. Initial letters of certain styles and patterns may effectively be used to "key" layouts in many interesting ways. The "contents" thumbnail at lower left is a possibility for an important page in a publication. The top left white panel is appropriate for the month's designation. The circular element at bottom suggests a spot for the logotype. The contents obviously would overprint the tinted area, provided the type size is sufficient for readability. If not, the tint could be eliminated. Practicability must be the first consideration in applying any design formula.

At the right a combination of tints give emphasis to an interestingly shaped "sky background" reverse that gives subtle emphasis to the building pattern which is counterbalanced at bottom left with a simple rectangular solid reverse heading.

In bottom left example, the horizontal "positive" element has angular sides which coincide with the left, angular side of the color screen tint which bleeds at three sides. A "key" for the proper angle should be the slant of the italic type used in the color band. The hand-lettered "subhead," which likewise could be one of the popular cursives or scripts, carries out the movement created by the other elements.

The bottom center flower motif shows a popular method of using a symbolic shape as a color background upon which a "positive" may be introduced.

The final layout illustrates the very effective manner in which a design becomes attractive by toning it contrastingly and accentuating both letters in the solid panel and the white spots on the palette by reversing them so the stock shows through. A little imagination in the choice of paper color would add immeasurably to the presentation. This design is activated by the interesting division of space caused by the curvilinear sweeps of the palette outline. Placement of the reverse spots in rhythmic progression carries the eye properly through the title at the right.

LIFE AT A TEA PARTY

Wolff crayon on smooth board. Halftone reproduction. Drawn by James Ryan.

Left—Pen and ink sketch. Line reproduction. *Above*—Pen and ink with stipple. Line reproduction. Drawn by James Ryan. (Two-color separation)

Pen and ink drawing with Ben Day shading

Wash drawing by May Burke. Drop-out highlight halftone.

Litho crayon drawing by Bernard Hirsch. Line reproduction.

Pen and brush drawing by George J. Tetzel

Scratchboard drawing by I. Doskow

Photography, Retouching, Art Work

SOME LAYOUT MEN may have ability in retouching, finished lettering, illustration or photography, but it is uncommon for one to be expert in all these phases. They are generally executed by artists who have developed distinctive techniques in their respective fields. It is essential, however, that the layout man have an intimate knowledge of art and photographic techniques so that he may specify them intelligently.

Photography is so encompassing as to constitute a profession in itself. However, the layout man may become proficient in specifying general photographic requirements through close association with proficient craftsmen and constant study of their techniques and products.

When given instructions for the taking of original photographs—the photographer should be furnished with a rough containing sketches of the pictures wanted in their exact layout dimensions or relative proportions; some indication as to definite objects, figures and details to be featured and those that may be subordinated; their tonal values; the style of backgrounds, and all other helpful specifications. He should be informed if color is to be introduced, what retouching and engraving techniques are to be employed, and of the printing procedures to be followed.

All other reproductive requirements should be carefully analyzed and the general copy theme and illustrative purpose of the pictures explained in detail, as the cooperation of the photographer in providing suitable background and lighting effects can materially reduce retouching costs and increase the attention value of the pictures. In many cases tonal values of objects in a picture and their contrast can be heightened considerably by the color and texture of background material. Various types and shades of characterful paper stock and other backgrounds may serve as colorful expedients to accentuate objects in a photograph.

Contact prints are seldom used for reproduction. Best results are obtained if an enlarged print is made from the negative, the chosen area retouched and then reduced again in making the photoengraving.

Glossy prints are best for reproduction, but where some particular technique of art rendering or retouching is to be employed, the photographs may be of a "mat" finish.

Photographs should be dry mounted on mat board to facilitate their handling and to prevent rolling, cracking or breaking. If they are to be cropped and mounted in combination with other pictures or art work, obviously they should be ordered unmounted.

Care should be exercised in handling and marking photographs for the engraver. Avoid using paper clips in attaching reproduction instructions. They may mark the copy. Do not write on the reverse of photos in pencil or pen. Indentations may show in the print. Use a china marking crayon in the white margins for this purpose.

Brief mention of the "silver print" process should be made here, as its application makes possible many unique treatments.

When a faithful line reproduction is wanted of a photograph, a light silver print is made from its negative. Upon this print the artist works in waterproof ink or grease crayon. When all sketching is completed, the print is immersed in a mercury bath which removes all photographic elements and leaves only the art work which is then reproduced as a line cut.

Retouching may be done on a photographic negative or on the print. The former requires the highest technical and artistic skill of the professional photographer and has rigid mechanical limitations. Most retouching of monotone pictures used in layout, therefore, is done on prints by painting and air-brushing with water colors. Every phase of retouching is a painstaking procedure and should be done only by a qualified artist who has access to the proper equipment. Discretion must be used in applying retouching to photographs as the photoengraver's camera is highly sensitive and retouching that is amateurishly done will show to disadvantage in the finished halftone.

Most fine detail in a picture requires retouching with a brush, but the delicately blended tone variances of a photograph require the use of an airbrush to blend the tones softly. Subjects with fine structural detail such as mechanical cross sections, pictures of machinery and other detailed elements must be minutely retouched, or not at all.

Retouching of portraits requires exceptional skill, and in most cases it should be avoided on facial features due to the possibility of distorting the subject's individual characteristics. The honesty of a photograph that is technically weak is always better than the artificiality of a highly retouched portrait that expresses no character or feeling.

A skilled photographer, achieving sharp contrast and effective detail, can simplify the task of retouching by carefully regulating highlights, shadows and the intermediate tones. Careful coordination of the work of these craftsmen is necessary to attain the utmost in graphic presentation.

Art work styles and techniques are practically unlimited. They may be classified briefly as pencil, crayon, pastel, ross board and charcoal sketches; pen and ink drawings; dry brush; tempera; wash and water color paintings; oil paintings. Each has its distinctive character, expressiveness and appropriateness to certain reproductive procedures.

The layout man should engage the services of competent artists who are specialists for all finished art work. Usually an illustrator cannot do lettering well, nor can a mechanical retoucher do justice to a figure sketch.

To know when and how to apply proper art work techniques is very essential and the layout man should study and evaluate the utmost possibilities and mechanical limitations of each style in order to save time and cost in reproduction.

A pen and ink drawing or a sketch rendered in dry brush, stipple, ross board or crayon, in which there are definite black elements such as lines, dots or solids, may be reproduced as a line cut. The tonal gradations of wash drawings and paintings, pencil, pastel and other similar techniques require halftone reproductions. Although the former styles may also be reproduced in halftone, the latter cannot be reproduced in line engravings. This is because the line process is incapable of retaining gray tone gradations, while the halftone process reproduces every detail. In reproducing line drawings by the halftone method, however, the entire area

111

occupied by the drawing will contain a background tone of halftone dots.

The layout man should be familiar also with highlight and vignette halftones and the varied offset and gravure reproduction techniques, as a comprehensive knowledge of these procedures and their relationship to paper and other mechanical requirements is essential in selecting the initial art technique.

The most essential requirement for good line reproduction is copy that is sharp and black. Drawings that are weak and contain gray and indecisive strokes will lose detail in reproduction. Use of a deep black waterproof ink is suggested in their rendering. Certain colors such as red, deep orange, and brown will reproduce like black. Most blues and purples will not reproduce unless the engraver uses a color filter. Light blue, therefore, may be used for guide lines and other markings and will drop out in photo-engraving.

Minor irregularities and crudities in pen and brush strokes are refined in reduction and for this reason drawings and sketches are usually made twice the size of the plate wanted.

Tissue paper overlays should be placed over all drawings, paintings, and retouched photographs to keep them clean and to prevent marring their original values. Size of engravings wanted, details of color separation and other instructions should be designated on the overlay.

To attain broad, even-tone values and delicate tone gradations without streaks, the air brush must be used. Parts of the picture that are not to be retouched must be masked.

Fine details on a photographic print require retouching with a brush. Some of the pencil and brush strokes in the illustrations of this volume were retouched as shown.

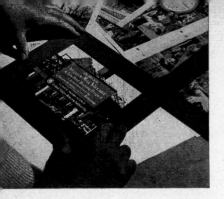

Cropping and Positioning Photographs

THE ATTENTION VALUE and illustrative qualities of all pictures can be increased tremendously by the diversified techniques of cropping, positioning and grouping. Fundamentally, one must develop a sound judgment of pictorial values and an appreciation for the subtle influences that make photographs effective.

If the layout man has the cooperation of a capable photographer in creating original pictures to fit a layout, he has a tremendous advantage, but in many cases he is furnished ready-made photographs from various sources of varying styles, tones, sizes and shapes. He must crop and position these pictures to accentuate their good features and subordinate or eliminate their unfavorable characteristics.

Skillful cropping is the initial expedient for making a photograph effective by trimming it of all unessential objects, superfluous details and detracting elements. Pictures may be cropped to horizontal or vertical rectangular shapes, circles, ovals and an unlimited variety of angular and curvilinear forms. They may also be silhouetted, vignetted, mortised, surprinted and combined in montages. They may be effectively accentuated by contrasting them against illustrative and decorative shapes and patterns, by cropping contours to stimulate objects, and by combining pictures with reverse plates, screen tint patterns and typographical accessories.

Before deciding on a definite shape for cropping, searching study should be made of the basic pictorial elements in a photograph, its composition, tone values, perspective, suggested motion and other influences to evaluate both the functional and illustrative suitability of the picture. Likewise, one should analyze carefully the copy theme and study the caption that may have been written for the picture.

Having determined the shape that will best emphasize the pictorial elements, the size relationship of the objects in the picture to the other

113

The two top elements in panel below are photoprints of snowflakes. They were transformed into negatives which were cut apart and cemented to form a design pattern which was, in turn, reversed in photoengraving and printed in color (bottom) for a Christmas greeting card.

This "collage" was achieved by silhouetting literally hundreds of pictures and parts of pictures and rubber-cementing them to form emphatic contrasts. It differs from a "montage" which is achieved by surprinting photographic negatives to blend together in a print which in turn is air brushed to refine hard edges and irregularities.

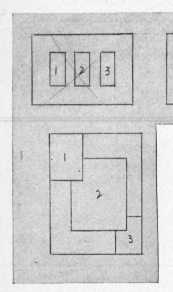

Dramatic, unusual silhouetting of pictures makes each of these ads an "eye stopper."

Simple outline sketches showing how three vertical pictures of a like size may be activated by changing size, shape, and position; also how changing the layout shape from a horizontal accentuates the vertical picture shapes. Top left—a static, uninteresting grouping of three elongated pictures. Top right—The picture shapes are cropped slightly and activated somewhat but the composition is still not accentuated enough. Bottom — a better composition which employs *proportion, balance, contrast, rhythm* and *unity* effectively.

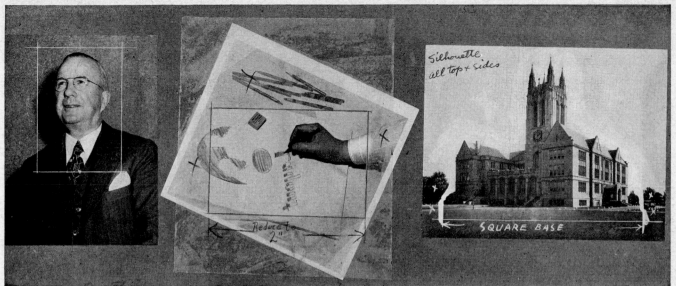

Above, the first example shows a portrait cropped to emphasize the essential area within the white rules. Second example shows how distracting elements, such as the pencils, may be eliminated by changing the angle of the cropping area. The desired rectangular area is drawn on tracing tissue, a frisket of this area cut out and the tracing placed over the photo. Third example shows definite silhouetting with white water color.

Right, "A Glimpse of America" layout emphasizes the broad horizontal nature of the pictures by bleeding them in that direction while the extreme right experimental pasteup accentuates the vertical qualities in the pictures.

In the bottom right panel, effective pictorial contrasts are achieved by proper cropping and placement.

Panel below shows how pictures may be cropped and silhouetted to shapes other than rectangular to accentuate a product or to suggest atmosphere.

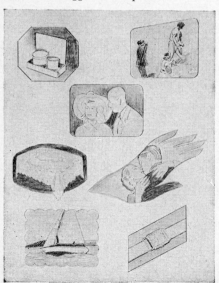

elements in the layout must be established to decide if an enlargement or reduction of the photo is required. Ofttimes layout proportions may be altered slightly to permit purposeful inclusion or elimination of some definite object or element in the picture, without upsetting the original layout scheme.

A set of masking angles is helpful in evaluating rectangular areas. These are two right-angular rules, which are placed together to form a rectangle, laid over the picture and manipulated until the correct area is chosen. The angles are helpful, also, in squaring a picture in which the horizontal or vertical elements are not photographically parallel to the outside edges.

Semi-transparent paper friskets may also be placed over a picture to evaluate various sizes and shapes for the photograph.

Cropping instructions for making rectangular photostats, photoprints or photoengravings may be given by making the cropping dimensions on the edges of the print with removable marking crayon, designating the dimensions with masking tape, or by placing a paper frisket or tracing paper over the entire photo and designating thereon the area to be reproduced. Silhouettes, vignettes and other irregular shapes may be outlined with white water color directly on a photograph or on a tissue overlay.

Mortises, Surprints and Backgrounds

When a photograph is used as a pictorial background for a mortise, the mortise should be shaped and positioned to utilize fully the illustrative and tonal values of the picture. It should be placed in an area of broad pattern, even tone and inconsequential detail and should contrast effectively yet pleasingly with the background. It should not conflict with any objects or details or obliterate any important pictorial elements. Neither should it blend into weak, monotonous tones in the background.

The pictorial background should subtly emphasize the purpose of the mortise and surround it with interesting and appropriate illustrativeness.

A mortise can be evaluated by cutting opaque paper to the desired size and shifting it on the photograph until the proper position is found.

116

Fundamentally, proper positioning and grouping of pictures is accomplished by applying the basic design requisites. For example, a photograph is correctly sized and shaped in relation to other elements if proportion and contrast are diligently applied. Balance is attained if the light and dark tones of the picture are properly related to other units and masses. Rhythm is stimulated if the attention-directing elements in a picture lead the eye in the proper direction.

Unity is exemplified by combining a picture with harmoniously related elements and grouping it with other units and masses in a unified pattern.

While pictures should be combined harmoniously, monotony in size, shape and tone should be avoided. Dimensions of certain pictures should be enlarged or reduced according to their display importance.

Horizontal and vertical shapes may be interestingly relieved by the use of irregular shapes, such as silhouettes, vignettes or circular forms.

Monotony in tone is avoided by placing photographs so that their dark, light and intermediary tones contrast effectively with each other. Photostatic enlargements or reductions of pictures may be cropped to fit a layout and then pasted in position. Thus definite dimensions are decided before costly engravings are ordered.

As the layout student progresses, he should acquire an appreciation of pictorial possibilities and a sound judgment of illustrative values. To augment this it is suggested that one constantly study the wide variety of techniques used in magazine and newspaper picture layout, as well as the treatments used in high-grade booklets, pamphlets and broadsides.

Who can resist the appeal of a baby picture? And what woman doesn't want lovely hair? Both vertical picture ads use their mortises to good advantage.

A two-page ad which uses forcefully silhouettes and contrastingly displayed pictures to full advantage. Note the effective "bridge-the-gutter" technique in both display type and optical carry-over of the phone wire.

Some examples of designing with circular shapes, silhouettes and panels.

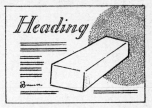

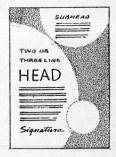

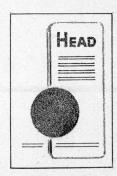

Author's sketches above illustrate the "new look" of modern layout patterns which employ interestingly shaped mortises on expansive tonal areas.

Two excellent advertisements which use well-proportioned and interestingly placed mortises. In the first example, three rectangular mortises contrast effectively with the silhouetted illustrative elements, while the oval mortise at the bottom points up the product name.

In the second example, the unconventional angles of the mortise and the partially rectangular reverse heading forcefully patterns an effective enclosure for the press silhouette.

Pictorial Perspectives

LAYOUTS THAT CONTAIN pictorial elements can be materially improved in effectiveness if the basic principles of linear perspective are forcefully applied in the preliminary shaping in thumbnails and emphatically accentuated in the finished photographs or drawings.

Our full appreciation of that desirable quality in a layout will broaden for us the scope of the five design requisites—*proportion, balance, contrast, rhythm* and *unity*—and will help us to master the unending possibilities for interesting space divisioning resulting from the variety of techniques in pictorial perspective.

While it is not our intention to delve deeply into complicated aspects of art, it seems desirable that the basic objectives of perspective, as outlined briefly in the accompanying sketches, should be understood, so that the monotony and stiltedness of "dead-on" shots and rigid rectangular photographs and art work may be avoided.

While the objective is to attain variety in shapes, lines and planes by avoiding the mathematical relationships in commonplace, unimaginative compositions, obviously the artificiality of overemphasized, exaggerated perspective so common in much of the so-called "modern" layouts should be avoided lest such distortion repel rather than attract and appeal. The naturalness and simplicity of sound perspective is to be desired rather than the grotesque or distorted.

In simple terms, the phenomenon of perspective as interpreted by the eye is translated somewhat as follows: The appearance of objects is changed and their dimensions are apparently distorted according to the various angles and distances at which they are visualized. That means that their sizes and shapes change according to the point from which they are viewed. These points of view may place an object directly ahead at a horizontal line of vision, or at various points above, below, to the left or to the right of the point of view.

To portray the apparent distortion of an object, such as the apparent visual decrease in size as it recedes from the eye, the dimensions furthest

119

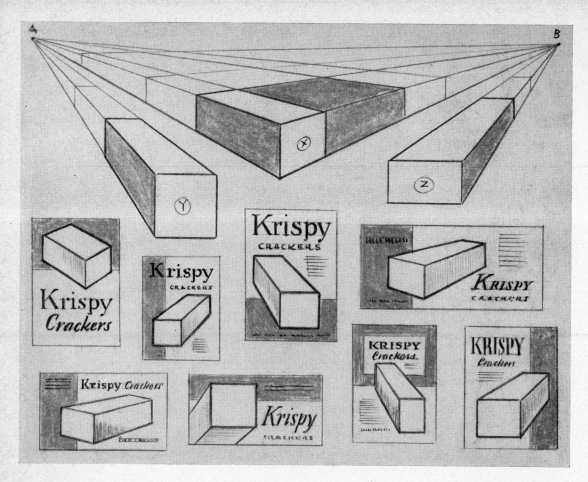

Left—In the top central examples (XYZ) of this panel, the phenomenon of perspective is basically illustrated with what are termed "systems" of lines. The left system lines converge at vanishing point A, and the right system at vanishing point B. The vertical lines throughout are parallel. The point of view is changed in each instance. These examples might be termed aerial perspective as the point of view is above the object.

In the eight thumbnails in the lower half of the panel, the perspective angles vary greatly, as does the point of view. The vanishing point of converging lines in each case would be at an imaginary spot far out of the layout area. By use of horizontal and vertical tint panels, the box becomes projected into the foreground in various forms of emphasis in relation to the heading and the text, which likewise vary in style and contrast according to the space patterns formed by the varying outlines and angles of the objects.

The three top sketches in the panel at right portray the apparent distortion of dimensions in perspective. For example, the width of the road as it converges in the distance, the height and width of the bridge and the same relative reduction in the proportions of the train. The television set is placed in a contrasting position with the rectangular horizontal panel to emphasize its perspective, likewise the lines of the "cake mix" package are pleasantly relieved by the circular lines of the cake in the foreground. The other sketches evaluate varying perspectives of objects in unusual placement. Note how the absolutely round face of the clock becomes distorted by perspective when viewed in a position other than face on.

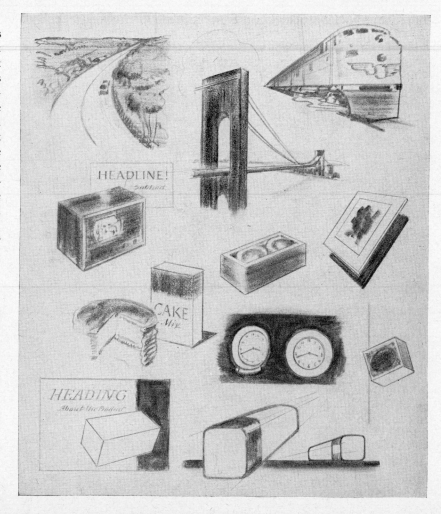

from the point of view must be reduced when drawing it on the tracing tissue. For example, a railway track going off into the horizon actually retains its same width but as it vanishes optically on the horizon the rails converge at an imaginary point known as the "vanishing point." Likewise, this same principle is carried out in the apparent optical distortion which reduces the height and width of an object which is furthest from the eye. Obviously, the distance of the vanishing point from the point of view regulates the angles of the object's silhouette.

The objectives of thumbnails and roughs containing interesting perspective are obvious: to find an angle at which the artist or photographer can produce a picture that has interesting shape, is non-mathematical in proportions, and which may be so placed in the layout that the remaining white space makes a practical pattern for the unhindered presentation of the message in type.

To make a detailed study of perspective in all its phases requires much more than the space at our disposal, and students who wish to elaborate should consult recognized texts.

It is hoped that by outlining the basic possibilities for attaining inviting layouts by the portrayal of pictorial elements in their most expressive perspectives the avoidance of the trite and commonplace in pictorial presentation will be accomplished.

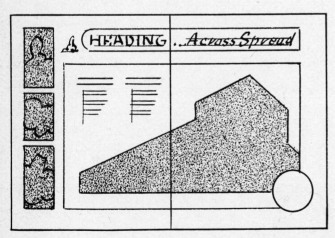

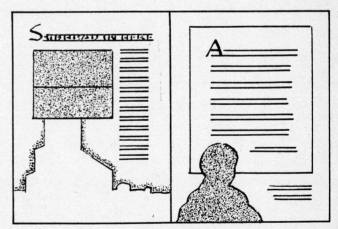

A pair of thumbnails for double-page spreads of a booklet, house organ or publication, wherein depth and perspective have been effectively introduced. In the first, the angular perspective of the central pictorial element "bridges the gutter."

In the second, illusion of depth is enhanced by placing the large silhouetted figure in the foreground at right and contrasting the building perspective far in the background, thus giving the upper left illustrative panel ample dominance.

Applying Hand Lettering
Initial Letters

WHEN INDIVIDUALITY is sought for a headline, signature, logotype, or other textual display unit, and it can not be readily attained with type, obviously it must be hand drawn. Limited use of appropriate lettering imparts individuality and artistic relief from the mechanical limitations of type. It "peps up" what might otherwise be an ordinary composition.

It is advisable, however, to explore thoroughly all the possibilities of available types before creating original lettering. Unless lettering is expertly rendered and its design advantages over type are indisputable, effectively composed type will better serve the purpose.

Each lettering style, through its structural characteristics, tone gradations, and other individual qualities, can convey a mood, suggest a definite atmosphere, and express a feeling. For example, a dainty script suggests grace and delicacy; the rugged Gothic or Old English style conveys a feeling of antiquity; the formal Roman form bespeaks conservatism and distinction; the sans-serif style interprets modernism.

While emphasis and contrast are desirable, care must be exercised to conform the lettering to the style and tone of the typography, and to the character of the other display elements.

Freakish lettering, which calls attention to itself more than to the message it portrays, should be avoided.

One should attain full artistic expressiveness and illustrative freedom when rendering lettering but a uniformity should be maintained in basic form and surface rendering, to accentuate the character of the style.

Lettering on a layout need not be rendered mechanically perfect in all details. Its draughtsmanship, however, should explicitly convey the desired style, tone and expressiveness.

The artist who makes the finished drawing for reproduction can refine any minor imperfections apparent in the layout.

Lettering may be adapted to reverse plates, screen tints, combination backgrounds and numerous other photoengraving techniques. It may likewise be combined with type, a photograph, trade-mark or other illustrative element.

One should cultivate a deep appreciation for the subtle qualities and influences inherent in various lettering styles.

Lettering styles and techniques continually change with typographical

A proof of a line of type is curved by slitting it between characters and cemented to fit a pattern for a screen tint background. This often obviates hand lettering.

Certain styles of initials must be drawn for reproduction, as shown in the upper left layout and finished drawing, but the practically unlimited variety of stock type initials offers the layout man a wide selection. The lower right layout utilizes a Raleigh cursive "N" with hand-drawn decoration.

Further showing of initial letters and lettering in layouts and finished form, demonstrating the preciseness with which the original creative lettering should be duplicated.

and layout trends, and the progressive layout man adapts each innovation in lettering as occasion demands. He scans continuously the pages of contemporary magazines that influence the trend so that by constantly increasing his lettering vocabulary he may become more versatile.

Initial Letters

The practice of using decorative initial letters is one of the oldest techniques in the graphic arts, stemming mainly from the works of the early scribes who illuminated book pages by hand.

The use of initial letters in modern layout has been more widely developed but the fundamental function of all initial letters is obviously the same—to attract the eye and direct interest to a desired point.

The size, weight and character of an initial letter should be regulated to conform harmoniously with the lettering, display type, text mass or other element with which it is to be combined. Likewise, the initial should be carefully positioned to insure continuity in reading the text that follows.

The choice of bulky, over-ornate or freakish initials or those whose character and style are not in harmony with its companionate elements should be avoided. Restraint is as advisable here as it is in the application of hand lettering and ornamentation.

Correctly chosen and properly placed initial letters can effectively accent rhythm by carrying the eye to display units in proper sequence. An initial letter may be used to combine display elements and promote unity. An initial letter may sometimes be used as the basic design element from which an entire layout evolves.

The possibilities for unusual treatments and applications of initial letters are practically endless. One should collect printed specimens of unusual techniques featuring initial letters for study and future adaptation to layouts.

As in applying hand lettering to a layout, one should not specify initial letters that require expensive art work and engravings for reproduction if comparable type initials are available or they can be constructed from typographic material.

When you know

An Attitude

your children

for the want

Christmas joys

Food for thought

Here is excitement

Typical examples of contemporary lettering in advertising and editorial layouts.

Thumbnails in the panel at right show the possibilities of initial letters in various forms of printed matter. The two top examples could be effected by using shaded initials composed "right out of the case" with stock rule or ornamentation. In the second from top left layout, the "d" is a combination of a sans serif "o" shaved at the right and a rule of comparative weight. The two initials in the roughs at the right are planned for hand lettering. The "kf" rough is another purely typographic arrangement, as is the "4 star" thumbnail. The "Copy" rough is calligraphic and requires hand lettering.

The "GI" layout would be applicable to a blotter and the "Yorke" thumbnail to a card. The last sketch might serve for the inside of a folder or a broadside.

These examples illustrate placement of initials for attention value, space divisioning and ornamentation.

Reproduction Proofs
Photoprints, Photostats

A REPRODUCTION PROOF is a printed facsimile of any typographical element or composition, from which photographic, photostatic, photoengraving, gravure or offset reproductions can be made. A reproduction proof can be used in actual size, enlarged or reduced to serve specific layout or reproductive purposes.

Usually, these proofs are printed clean and sharp on finely coated paper to insure faithful reproduction of all detail such as letter serifs, fine lines, shading and other elements. Reproduction proofs also may be made from over-inked type or cuts on rough, antique stock, to appear ragged purposely and convey an antique effect for specialized layout purposes.

Reproduction proofs are employed in making line cuts, reverse plates, combination engravings and those of varying screen tint backgrounds in every conceivable size and shape. They may be surprinted on drawings, maps, charts and photographs. They may also be photostated or photoprinted in various sizes to evaluate type styles and certain layout techniques on roughs before costly photoengravings are made.

Reproduction proofs of type are often used in conjunction with art work to form novel designs and to eliminate costly hand lettering.

There is a wide technical distinction between a photoprint and a photostat. A photoprint is produced by taking a picture of a reproduction proof, drawing or other pictorial subject on a photographic negative and making a print from it. It more closely approximates the original subject than does the photostat, the print of which is made from a paper negative.

Photoprints are more costly than photostats and take longer to produce but their use is advocated where accurate reproduction is wanted. They reproduce minute details faithfully while photostats do not.

While a photostat may become slightly distorted due to uncontrollable stretch or shrinkage in making it, it generally suffices for visualization purposes in the average layout. Photostats of type proofs or lettering may be reproduced in photoengraving, either as positives (black on white) or negatives (white on black) where minor deviations from the original are inconsequential or where cost is a factor.

Photostats are often made from complete layouts in sufficient number to facilitate simultaneous mechanical production in various departments, and to preserve original visuals.

Photostats for layout purposes may often be made from certain objects, provided they can be placed in proper focus before the photostat camera. These photostats, however, cannot be used for reproduction because they lack tone and detail.

With an intimate knowledge of reproductive processes and skill in the manipulation of reproduction proofs, photoprints and photostats, the layout man with a fertile imagination can achieve many unique effects.

From the original drawing at *top left* an enlarged photostatic negative was made, which, when combined with art work, produced panel at lower left. The die-cut head of Franklin at bottom was reproduced from a positive made from the original negative and photoengraved with the reversed type lines. The two-color lace patterns on Polaris cover at right was achieved with photostat negatives and positives of embossed paper patterns, engraved with the other elements.

Below—The letter "K" in three experimental photoprint enlargements, both negative and positive. *Bottom left*—A photoprint enlargement is made of a certain portion of a smaller, more expansive original print. *Top right*—tracing paper placed over a photoprint with a reproduction proof of type placed in accurate position for combination with photoprint in engraving. *Lower right*—the larger, original photoprint is reproduced by means of a silverprint over which a pen drawing was made and the print bleached. By this means certain elements may be added or eliminated.

Photoengraving
Other Reproductive Processes

THERE ARE THREE basic processes for reproducing graphic material in print.

Relief, or letterpress, as it is commonly known, is the printing directly from type, photoengravings, electrotypes and other plates, the printing surfaces of which are raised above the base. It is the most simplified form of printing and is the most widely used.

Planograph, as its name implies, is the method of printing from a plane, or even surface on which a photographic image is etched. It includes lithography, offset, multilith and photo gelatin printing.

Intaglio, is the method of printing directly from plates which have the subject matter etched below the surface. Gravure, rotogravure, steel and copper plate engraving are in this classification.

In order not to confuse the layout student, we will avoid any exhaustive technical discourse on the mechanical phases of each process and suggest that he familiarize himself primarily with the possibilities and limitations of each process.

As the relief process is most generally used, we will briefly analyze the various types of photoengraving as they apply to letterpress printing.

Photoengraving is the method of reproducing drawings, paintings, photographs, maps, type proofs and other copy by photographing on a sensitized negative which in turn is printed on a sensitive copper or zinc plate. The plate is then etched with chemicals so that the printing image remains above the etched part. The finished plate is made type-high by blocking on wood or metal.

Basically there are two kinds of photoengravings—the *line cut* and the *halftone.*

The *line cut* is the simpler to produce and is less costly than the halftone. It reproduces pen and ink drawings, maps, charts, reproduction proofs and other copy which is clearly defined in one tone of black or in

128

any one color that reproduces black. As its name implies, the printing plate is an exact duplicate of the lines, solids and other detail in the copy, which may either be enlarged or reduced.

The average line cut is made on zinc, but for fine work with great detail copper is used, because it etches cleaner and sharper.

Mechanical shadings, known as Ben Day screens, may be applied to line cuts in a wide variety of tones.

Line copy may also be reversed to appear white on black and on screen backgrounds. These are known as "positives." Black on a screen tint is a "surprint."

Line cuts may be made for printing two or more colors, each color necessitating a separate engraving.

Copy must be furnished separated for each color as the camera cannot separate multicolored copy for line work.

The *halftone* reproduces photographs, washdrawings, paintings, and all copy which has variable gradations of tone. Copy is photographed through a screen which breaks it up into a succession of small dots of variable sizes. The dots interpret the tone values of the original on the negative and in turn on the finished plate. The etching and finishing processes are basically the same as for the line cut, but the finished plate has a screen-like surface overall.

Varying paper surfaces require a wide range of halftone screens. The coarsest is made 50 lines to the inch, for use on rougher antique and newspaper stock, and the finest is 250 line screen for printing on the highest surfaced paper obtainable. The finest screen advisable for good commercial printing on coated stock is usually 133 lines to the inch.

They are generally known in the trade as 50 screen, 60 screen, 80 screen and so on.

When in doubt as to proper screen, the photoengraver should be consulted and given a sample of the paper to be printed.

Halftones are generally rectangular, but they may also be oval, circular, silhouetted or vignetted to any desired shape.

The highlight halftone is one in which the dots in highlights and other light elements of washdrawings or pencil sketches are toned down or dropped out entirely so no screen appears in these areas.

The combination plate is a combination of line and halftone negatives superimposing and printed as one plate.

Multi-colored copy, such as an oil painting, water color or Kodachrome, is reproduced in full color by the four color process. The colors are yellow, red and blue with black plate, which is usually the "key plate." The copy is separated by use of color filters and a halftone plate for each color is made. Multi-colored copy may also be reproduced in three colors—yellow, red and blue.

Duotones are two-color halftone engravings made from colored copy such as tinted photographs, and two-color washdrawings.

Left—Type of multi-tone copy, suitable for halftone engraving, including silhouettes, vignettes and combination engravings. Colored copy of this type is suitable for duotone and color-process engraving.

The art work at bottom center was produced by the airbrush which furnishes the engraver soft, feather-edge copy.

Below—Type of definitely black and white copy suitable for "line" engravings. Note the careful marking of engraving instructions on each.

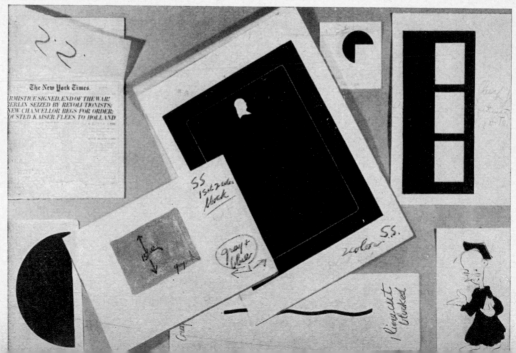

Specimen sheets of screen tints and Ben Day screens, for guidance in specifying, are available from your photoengraver.

The top photograph has a paper frisket, or mask, placed over it to guide the engraver in securing the proper area and angle. The lower illustrates how removable masking tape may also be used.

Duographs are two-color halftones made from monotone pictures, the second color being produced by photographing at two different angles.

There are many other types of intermediate plates which may be produced by the combination of or adaptation of the foregoing styles. Color prints, for instance, may be made by using solid line colors or screen tints printed transparently over black halftones or line plates. Likewise in monotone engravings, an almost unlimited variety of techniques and procedures is possible. It is advisable, however, for the layout student to acquire a thorough knowledge of all these processes before specifying them. The alternative is to seek the guidance of a competent photoengraver.

As offset and gravure are both photographic processes employing the same general principles as photoengraving, art and illustrations are prepared basically the same. There are many limitations and advantages in each method, however, and the student is advised to acquire specialized reference books for study of the wide range of reproductive processes.

131

Preparation of copy for offset reproduction is shown at the right. At top left is the rough of a center spread in a broadside. In the center is the outline drawing with halftone areas designated and type proofs pasted in position. At lower right is the completed printing. In upper right is shown the illustration and type paste-up for the front cover and a reversed reproduction of same.

The predominating element in the panel below is a large offset reproduction in several colors on a piece of satin. This type of illustrative copy is ideal for offset. The smaller unit at the bottom is a sample of sheet-fed gravure, also an ideal process for pictorial presentations.

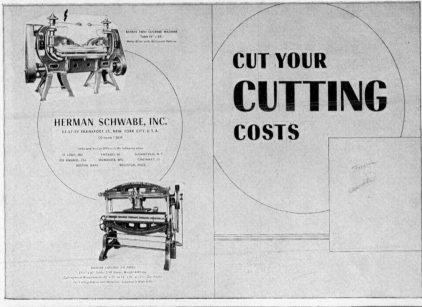

Examples at right are the actual-size "mechanical" at top and the finished offset reproduction which it guided. Note lines designating color areas and positioning for "strip-ins," also photostats pasted in position for proper placement of pictures. Reproduction proofs of type are in exact position.

A Short Study of Types...
Their Functions

THE STUDY OF TYPE and its many forms and functions is so highly specialized that its evaluation in a work of this kind is necessarily limited. We therefore confine ourselves to a brief analysis of the basic type styles, the underlying principles that impart individuality to type, govern its selection and make its use practical and efficient from a layout standpoint.

Type, which interprets the fullest functions of lettering in a mechanical way, likewise can express atmosphere and impart definite character and feeling. It can also emphasize the physical construction and expressiveness of a layout and the message it portrays. Thousands of styles make type adaptable to any subject or manner of presentation.

The layout student should familiarize himself with the origin and evolution of the basic type styles which are classified as: Gothic Text, Old Style, Transitional, Modern, Sans Serif, Square Serif, Script, Cursive and Contemporary.

Gothic Text is the original type style originated by Gutenberg. It was derived from the hand-lettering of that era. It has a highly decorative character and bespeaks reverence and antiquity. It should be used sparingly, mainly for display, in layouts of a scholarly or ecclesiastical nature. The distinguishing characteristics of Gothic Text are its heavy body forms which terminate in sharp tapering curves and angles. The contrasting thin elements of the letters accentuate the ornateness of the style. Some examples are: Goudy Text, Cloister Black and Old English.

Old Style, which interprets the original classical Roman design, was created to impart more legibility and flexibility to the great volume of printing that followed Gutenberg's invention. It served also to coordinate the style of printing with the style of lettering used for stone inscriptions.

Old Style has limitless interpretations in both display and text and

133   **PART SEVEN**

offers the layout man a most versatile design with which to work. It is characterized by a graceful transformation of body weights from heavy to light and has serifs that are curved and slanting. Some examples of this style are Caslon, Garamond, and Goudy. Old Style types print best on antique papers for which they were originally created.

Modern style types are structurally the same as Old Style, stemming basically from the classical Roman also, but differing in serifs and surface form. This style was originated by Bodoni and extended further the structural design possibilities of the basic Roman forms. The chief characteristics of the Modern style are evident in the abrupt termination of the evenly-shaped verticals against thin right-angular serifs and a decided contrast between the thick and thin curved body elements of the letters. The leading examples of this style are Bodoni, Mondial and Onyx. They can be printed best on hard surfaced paper.

Types such as Bulmer, Scotch Roman and Baskerville, whose serifs are of an intermediate character between Old Style and Modern are known as *Transitional* types because they typify the transition from the Old Style to Modern. The text of this volume is set in 14 pt. Linotype Baskerville leaded 4 points.

Sans Serif styles follow Roman forms, but as the name implies, are entirely devoid of serifs, and the body weight is mainly uniform throughout. The style was originated in comparatively recent years when revolutionary changes in layout and design techniques demanded a more simplified, streamlined type style. Prominent among the Sans Serif types are Futura, Kabel, and Bernhard Gothic.

Square Serif styles follow the basic Roman structure but the relative alikeness of surface weight of body and serifs warrants their separate classification. Some examples are Stymie, Girder and Beton.

Script styles are based on decorative handwriting forms. Stemming from the slanting style of lettering used in illuminating by hand, script has developed into many free flowing interpretations. Its ornateness forbids its extensive use and it is used mainly to add a decorative touch. The thin strokes which tie the letters together forbid letter spacing. The style is exemplified by Typo Script, Commercial and Trafton Script.

Cursive styles are derivatives of Script and Italic styles, combining certain characteristics of each. Cursive must also be used sparingly, and should not be letter spaced. Some examples are Bernhard Cursive, Coronet and Mozart.

Contemporary styles are unusual creations which do not fit precisely into any of the above classifications but through their novel characteristics should be grouped independently. The style is exemplified by Lydian, Eve, Cartoon and many other current faces.

Each type style has definite design characteristics which are evident in the construction and form of certain letters and which distinguish it from other styles. The decided shape, curve or angle of a serif, the slant of a cross bar or the contour of a body element makes a certain type style distinctive and individual.

To familiarize himself thoroughly with these characteristics, the layout student will find it advantageous to trace and copy letters from type specimen books.

Many type faces are available in both light and bold face, and are usually accompanied by an italic interpretation which retains the main design characteristics of the font but is designed on a slanting angle. This variance from the horizontal form of the Roman gives italic emphasis, accentuation, motion and other qualities of expressiveness.

Some faces are available in medium and extra bold face also.

Best results are obtained in layout by limiting type styles and sizes to a minimum. The experienced typographer knows what types can be combined harmoniously, but it is well for the layout student to limit his choice to one good series of type in a layout and achieve variety and interest by an intelligent use of accentuating forms, shapes and sizes. Practice will enable one eventually to combine various styles, but good taste and suitability should always dictate the choice.

Weight of type for text masses should be specified carefully to achieve the correct tone value and to accomplish proper contrast and harmony with headlines and other display elements. Skillful use of word and letter spacing, paragraph indentions, and leading between lines influence tone values of type masses. Types of the lighter and medium tone are read more easily in a mass than the heavy types. The mechanical adaptability of all type styles should be fully explored before definitely specifying their use. Type prints darker on soft antique paper than on smooth coated stock. Type that has fine hairlines or shaded elements should be printed on hard surfaced stock to bring out all detail clearly.

Reading of type under varying conditions of light and by dissimilar audiences is an important factor, and type sizes for text masses should be chosen accordingly. A study of text masses, in general, will disclose that 9 or 10 point type is most suitable for text masses in publications and pamphlets. Type style, width of line, page size and many other conditions alter this generality, however.

When selecting type for lengthy text masses one should not choose a particular style because of the pronounced design characteristics of the larger display sizes. The appearance and effectiveness of a type style in a mass should rather be evaluated from specimens set in the text sizes.

Modern typographers usually supply specimen sheets showing display and text types set in varying widths and degrees of leading, from which a quick evaluation can be made. Such specimen sheets are invaluable also for ascertaining character count when computing copy in relation to space.

Type should not be set in too wide a measure, as there is a theoretical limit to what the eye can read comfortably. A general rule is to set text type in a width of not more than two times its alphabet length.

Types like Forum, Empire and Huxley Vertical are made in capitals only and they necessarily demand a different technique than do the Gothic Text types such as Old English, or Goudy Text which are illegible and unsightly if set in capitals alone.

Some type designs can be leaded more freely than others, due to variations in weight, size of the body and difference in length of lower case ascenders and descenders.

Certain even-toned type styles lend themselves well to photoengraving and other reproductive techniques while others with fine lines or delicate characteristics should be avoided. Reducing or enlarging type or combin-

ROMAN CAPS and lower case

ITALIC CAPS and lower case

Script Caps and lower case

Gothic text Caps and lower case

BETON Light

BETON Medium

BETON Bold

BETON Extra Bold

Cheltenham Bold

Chelt. Bold Exten

NEWS GOTHIC

NEWS GOTHIC CONDENSED

NEWS GOTHIC EXTRA CONDENSED

---

36 pt. Nicholas Cochin

36 pt. Caslon 471

36 pt. Caslon 540

36 pt. Mondial Bold

(Types reduced in engraving)

Basic type structures

At left are the four basic type structures from which all of our type styles evolve. Each has many variations and adaptations in surface rendering but all stem from these basic forms.

Type weights

Many types are made in light and bold, some also in medium, but few in all of the weights here illustrated. Types like this and Futura offer the widest possible tone range for layout purposes.

Type widths

As practicability demands variable tones for emphasis, so does the layout man often use type structures that are expanded or condensed, to fit certain patterns.

Type heights

Type designs in a given point size may vary considerably in height of printing surface. This is due to the variation of the main body height and the length of ascenders such as in d, f, h, k, l, t, and descenders such as in g, j, p, q and y.

Masculine——*Feminine*

Antique——Modernistic

Serious——*Frivolous*

BULKY——*Delicate*

Dignified——*Carefree*

Monotoned——SPIRITED

POSTERY——*Sketchy*

Reserved——*Relaxed*

Expressibility

This cross-section of type styles available in a modern composing room illustrates the wide range of expressibility in the various forms. The type used in each instance should not form any pre-conceived ideas in the mind of the layout student regarding mandatory use.

The use of certain styles above should be limited to display purposes and then only with the proper text type.

Below—This style of basic letter construction is a sound pattern for designating the average Roman type faces on roughs, because it has an ample fullness and character which typifies the general Roman structure. Surface characteristics such as style of serif, change in body weight and other variances may be added when the pattern is completed and the definite type chosen.

For proportionate dimensions of the characters not shown the same general width and height classifications described in the chapter on lettering may be followed.

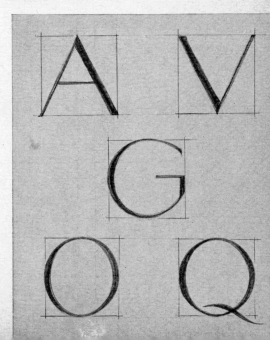

ing it with screen tints necessitates careful selection of type style for proper accentuation.

Type for reverse plates should be of a bolder face than for regular use, as dark backgrounds tone the value of the reverse lettering considerably.

The layout man should be alert to changes in typographical trends and must keep pace with improvements in type design and manufacture. He should know the limitations of hand composition in mass production and should specify Linotype, Intertype, Monotype, Ludlow or other machine composition when practicability demands it.

Practical experience as a compositor is the soundest background for acquiring a knowledge of the mechanics of typography. Lacking this, the layout student should avail himself of every opportunity to visit composing rooms and study at first hand the mechanical procedures so that he may specify them efficiently. Likewise, he should read specialized textbooks on the subject.

Good typography does not stem from imagination and originality alone, but from a combination of these qualities with an intimate knowledge of sound craftsmanship and a reverence for types and their functions.

A reproduction of two facing pages of Gutenberg's famous bible. This is credited with being the first printing from movable type. Bible was set in a Gothic Text style which has long since been discarded for continuous reading, in our language.

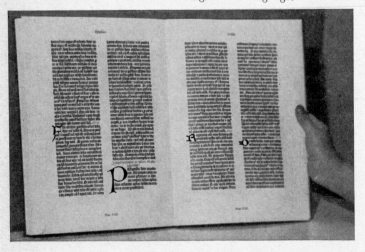

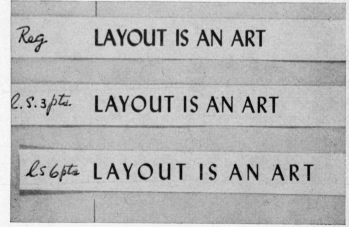

Above—Three differently-spaced lines showing the effect that letter spacing has on the tone and readability of a display line. The introduction of proper white space between letters slows up the reading somewhat but helps the eye assimilate the design of the lettering and softens the tone of closely-fitted letters. Widely letter spaced lines are used mainly to achieve some design function and should be avoided in the normal composition of headings.

Text

Layouts embodying Gothic Text generally should be formal in structure. Illustrations rendered in the traditional woodcut style are most appropriate. Elaborate ornamentation, decorative initials and embellishments can accompany Gothic Text. The display and text types used with Gothic Text should be Old Style, preferably those of the heavier faces. The serifs of Old Style will harmonize with the curved and tapered thin strokes of Gothic Text.

Two distinctive ads of contrasting layout style and typography. Both attain attractiveness, individuality and proper tone accompaniment to the illustration by using in each case one-family typography. The informally balanced ad, left, combines the Modern style types. Ultra

Bodoni and Onyx (a Bodoni derivative) with Bodoni for text. The formally balanced ad, right, is entirely in Caslon, an Old Style type. Note the absence of ornamentation in the informal layout as contrasted with the decorative border in the formal layout at the right.

Old S

Having characteristics of traditional pen lettering, Old Style types are the logical choice for layouts of a traditional, conventional, dignified and reserved nature. They harmonize with sketchy pen and ink, pencil or wash drawings and halftones that have soft delicate characteristics. Accompanying ornamentation may be flowery and decorative.

Tran N

Transitional types, when used in text, may safely be combined with sound display faces of another classification. The Transitional style, exemplifying certain characteristics of both Old Style and Modern, harmonizes well with illustrations and ornamentation applicable to both Old Style and Modern. Its intermediate character makes it a safe choice for both display and text when type combinations are contemplated.

Mod Ital

Stemming from the engravers' tool and embodying its characteristics — a more simplified, mechanical evenness of surface design and angularity of serifs — Modern types may be combined with many of the Sans Serif and Contemporary types, in both formal and informal arrangements. Modern faces harmonize with halftones and illustrations of broad, strong pattern and contrasting values. Ornamentation should accentuate the simplified contours of the letters and the angularity of serifs.

SAN

Rev

The simplicity of line and form, which stems from the rule and compass, makes Sans Serif faces adaptable to the wide variety of informal layouts which are mainly patterned by rectangular divisions of space and structural elements that have simplified contours, Sans Serif harmonizes with halftones of broad, contrasting values and may be successfully incorporated in a diversified variety of screen tint patterns and reverse plates; also with illustrations of monotone lines, flat areas and simplicity of rendition. If rules and ornamentation are employed, they must accentuate and characterize the unadorned simplicity of the style.

Sans Serifs may be successfully used for various forms of display, for subheads, captions and lead-ins and when there is a limited amount of text in a type mass. Experience has shown that, for lengthy text matter, Modern or Transitional styles such as Caledonia or Baskerville are more readable than Sans Serif.

Brush

CARTOON
✗

Flat

Rug...

Square Serif faces, also termed Egyptian or "Flat Serif," due to their strong structural qualities, are used mainly to emphasize patterns of like nature, and to strengthen the many types of so-called "modern" layouts, typified by informal, rectangular divisions of space and allocation of elements. Illustrations and halftones should be keyed to the tone of the type weight and should emphasize the simple ruggedness of the Square Serif style. Ornamentation should obviously accentuate the monotone qualities of the type style.

Script & Cursive

Script harmonizes with delicately rendered pen and ink sketches, etchings, certain types of pencil and wash drawings, drop-out highlight halftones or sketchy line and halftone combinations. Ornamentation should accentuate the thick and thin curved elements of Script and be keyed to the variable weights of the different styles. A more ornate tempo in decoration is permissible with Script than with the more rugged Roman structures.

Either Old Style, Modern or Transitional text faces would be appropriate to accompany display set in Script depending on the Script style and the style of the layout. A traditional pattern utilizing Commercial Script for display would suggest text type such as Garamond Oldstyle. Conversely, a smart, informal

Playbill }

Due to the complexity of design in this group, no general formula for their application can be established. Some Contemporary faces are of Old Style origin while others typify the Modern. Some designs have characteristics that embody several styles. For example, Lydian may be said to be "Sans Serif," yet it has the thick and thin variations inherent in Old Style. It also has certain calligraphic qualities of Gothic Text without the decorative embellishments.

arrangement suggests the up-to-date Trafton Script and a Modern text face such as Bodoni Book or Caledonia. Transitional text type, such as Weiss, harmonizes with either Script display style.

The same general principles regarding illustrations, ornamentation and accompanying text style that pertain to Script are applicable likewise to Cursive.

Monotone Scripts like Kaufman Script, Signal and the variable-tone heavy Brush more definitely fit into the Contemporary classification than into the category of delicate scripts previously described. From this it will be seen that a sort of "catch-all" classification termed "Contemporary" is necessary to obviate the endless breakdown of type classifications.

Summary of the Origin and Development of Leading Styles

Historically speaking, the types of Claude Garamond are credited with being the first roman and italic fonts to displace the Gothic Text and other calligraphic forms early in the 16th century. In this transformation it was logical for Garamond to retain some of the pen characteristics in the design of his classical French face. For example, he used the well rounded, tapered serifs, graceful thick and thin variations in verticals, diagonals and curved strokes, together with many other subtle handlettering niceties to transform the basic classical Roman skeleton form that had previously been used for stone inscriptions into a more graceful vehicle for the printing of the charming title pages for books and other classical literature on the antique, hand-made printing papers contemporary with him.

The Functions of Old Style

These main identifying Old Style characteristics have been dominant in the design of all subsequent Old Style types and our purpose is to evaluate a few of the better known types in this category, so that their layout function may better be understood.

The present-day Garamond and the Garamont (a typecasting appellation) fonts which have received such

widespread recognition because of their versatility, subtle tone variances and good relationship to many forms of reproduction, are derivatives of the original Garamond fonts. They have been technically refined and elaborated to fit modern typecasting and typesetting techniques which improved their versatility, without deviating materially from the original design.

The adaptability of the Garamond "family" to modern layout techniques and their suitability for printing on both antique and smooth stocks is well proven by their consistent use in outstanding current advertisements.

The French gracefulness and elegance inherent in Garamond is characterized by the clearness and openness of the curved letters, the well set-up verticals and diagonals, based on nicely rounded, ample serifs which are not as sharp or pointed as in Caslon or Janson. In the capitals, such as the "A," the cross bars are high; the "T" has top left and right serifs of differing slants. In the lower case, both "a" and "e" have unusually small counters. Long ascenders and descenders add grace and charm to a small, main lower case body which is legible with a minimum of leading.

Janson was the next prominent type designer, in the 17th century. The

heavier, rounder, more definitely thick and thin, sharper-serifed Janson type which he created has a well-proportioned Dutch sturdiness which fits it ideally for the more rugged layout structures where a darker tone and more forceful text areas are desired. Janson capitals are full, and well-proportioned. They have a ruggedness which is contrasted by the relatively thin cross bars and sharp meeting points of the diagonals.

Next in historical sequence is Caslon who started his foundry in 1720 in England.

This simple, clear, ideally-proportioned type face which symbolizes the traditional Old Style by its rounded, sharp pointed serifs and its graceful transformation from thick to thin has often been referred to as the one type that will never be superseded for all-around serviceability.

Strong, masculine layout patterns and delicate, dainty, feminine effects are equally attainable with Caslon, depending upon the choice of letter form, size, letter spacing and leading.

The variances of the original Caslon font are many as this face has been adapted to every means of type founding and typecasting machines. One main characteristic that remains obvious in every interpretation is the

GARAMONT 248

This is 72-point Garamont	*This is 72-point Garamont Italic*
Bright	*Foreign*
This is 60-point Garamont	*This is 60-point Garamont Italic*
Popular	*Identities*
This is 48-point Garamont	*This is 48-point Garamont Italic*
Distinctly	*Inky Dregs*
This is 42-point Garamont	*This is 42-point Garamont Italic*
Impersonal	*Clean Edges*
This is 36-point Garamont	*This is 36-point Garamont Italic*
Is Perfection	*Prints Legibly*
This is 30-point Garamont	*This is 30-point Garamont Italic*
Superior Finish	*Compare Texture*

GARAMOND BOLD 548

This is 72-point Garamond Bold	*This is 72-point Garamond Bold Italic*
Sturdy	***Testing***
This is 60-point Garamond Bold	*This is 60-point Garamond Bold Italic*
Opacity	***Uniform***
This is 48-point Garamond Bold	*This is 48-point Garamond Bold Italic*
NoLumps	***Long Fibre***

A SPECIMEN of Janson Type

ABCDEFGHIJKLMNOPQRSTUVWXYZ&abcdefghijklmnopqrstuvwxyz fiffl .,;-'!?()*†§ $1234567890

*ABCDEFGHIJKLMNOPQRSTUVWXYZ& abcdefghijklmnopqrstuvwxyzfiffl .,;-'!? () *†§ $1234567890*

ABCDEFGHIJKLMNOPQRSTUVWXYZ&abcdefgh ijklmnopqrstuvwxyzfiffl.,;-'!?()*†§ $1234567890

ABCDEFGHIJKLMNOPQRSTUVWXYZ& abcdefghij klmnopqrstuvwxyzfiffl.,;-'!?()†§ $1234567890*

ABCDEFGHIJKLMNOPQRSTUVWXYZ&ÆŒ abcdefghijklmnopqrstu vwxyzæœfiffl.,;-'!?()*†§ $1234567890

ABCDEFGHIJKLMNOPQRSTUVWXYZ&ÆŒ abcdefghijklmnopqrstuvwxyz æœfiffl.,;-'!?()†§ $1234567890*

ABCDEFGHIJKLMNOPQRSTUVWXYZ&ÆŒabcdefghijklmnopqrstuvwxyzæœfiffl .,;-'!?()*†§ $1234567890

ABCDEFGHIJKLMNOPQRSTUVWXYZ&ÆŒ abcdefghijklmnopqrstuvwxyz æœ fiffl .,;-'!?()†§ $1234567890*

ABCDEFGHIJKLMNOPQRSTUVWXYZ&ÆŒabcdefghijklmnopqrstuvwxyzæœabcdefghijklmn opqrstuvwxyzæœfiffl.,;-'!?()*†§ $1234567890

*ABCDEFGHIJKLMNOPQRSTUVWXYZ&ÆŒ abcdefghijklmnopqrstuvwxyzæœ fiffl .,;-'!? () *†§ $1234567890*

capital A, in which the top of the heavy right diagonal downstroke projects over the top of the left diagonal and forms a curving line as if a "bite" were taken out of the top.

The remarkable success that Caslon attained seems to have outshone succeeding type founders until Baskerville's time.

We must bring our evaluation of Old Style types up to date by mention of that great disciple of tradition, the late Fred Goudy, who designed 121 type faces, notable among them, Goudy Old Style, Kennerley, Hadriano and Forum Title. Fred Goudy died in 1947.

Goudy adhered principally to the traditional Old Style forms and created new interest in his types by varied modifications of tone, weight, movement and character of serifs.

Major Surface Style Changes

Just as the alert type designer, typographer and printer of today constantly seeks improved typographic devices with which to create new and more effective compositions, so were the printing craftsmen of the 18th century aware of the need for more versatility in the design of the type faces at their disposal.

Many calligraphers and type designers were endeavoring to change the classical Roman Old Style structure in appearance so as to give added variety, wider scope and greater artistic influence to the Roman form which by then had replaced Gothic Text forms throughout most of Europe. These changes were mainly slight transformations of surface characteristics and subtle variations in the proportions of the letters.

An outstanding English calligrapher, John Baskerville, who was inspired by the success of Caslon, created the type which bears his name.

Baskerville, which is known as an outstanding example of the Transitional style by its tendency to precision and exactness (a quality not inherent in Caslon and many Old Style types) may be said to have foreshadowed the creation of the definitely original Modern Style created about a half century later by Giambattista Bodoni in Italy.

The classification "Transitional" is given to Baskerville and types of similar character because they typify that period of design transition from the curved, slanting, tapering characteristics of the original Old Style types to the mathematical preciseness, classical formality, originality and evenness that typifies Bodoni and all subsequent Modern types of similar character.

The Transitional Style, having some of the characteristics of both Old Style and Modern, may safely be combined either in text or display with either, but good typographic practice forbids the combining of Old Style and Modern because their surface characteristics are not in harmony.

Baskerville has a decided roundness and openness which, together with its delicacy, makes it particularly readable in text masses. Its evenness in mass exerts a uniform gayness of tone.

Like the Old Style Garamond and the Modern Bodoni, Baskerville has been adapted to every form of typecasting machine and, in the main, has not deviated from Baskerville's original design.

The italics, particularly the foundry and Monotype versions, have a full-flowing characteristic that enhances readability, a quality often lost in italic interpretations.

Another outstanding Transitional style is ATF's Bulmer, which enjoys great popularity for display. At present it is available for hand composition only. As with Baskerville, Scotch Roman and other Transitional faces, it may be combined effectively with almost any Old Style or Modern text face.

The Weiss types available in both light and bold, together with the inimitable Weiss initials offer the layout man and typographer one of the most versatile Transitional faces with which

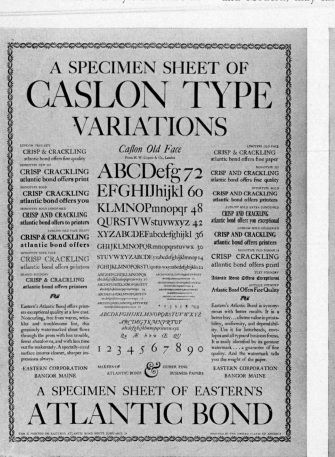

to construct gracious looking typography. The dignified classicism of Weiss types imparts rugged solidity and vigor or extreme delicacy to a layout, depending upon its usage. Its italic is unusually graceful and reminiscent of calligraphy at its best.

Bodoni Created Modern Style

Our evaluation of Bodoni as the leading exponent of the Modern style would not be complete without mentioning the extensiveness of this type family. Bodoni book is the lightest version. More weight is achieved in the "regular" Bodoni and blackness is definitely imparted to a page by the use of Bodoni Bold. With the introduction of the Utra Bodoni, Poster Bodoni and Onyx (a Bodoni derivative) for display, an extreme blackness in both expanded and condensed type styles is possible.

These darker versions should be used with caution lest they demonstrate the axiom that "all display is no display" in the compositions that employ them for emphasis.

Obviously, bolder types when set in text masses, require ample leading. Due to their relatively thin serifs, Bodoni and other Modern faces should be used cautiously in reverse plates and as surprints on screen tinted backgrounds. The transitional styles are better suited for such usage because of a more solidly constructed serif which graduates into a slight curve in its meeting with the heavy vertical. The meeting points of crossbars, verticals and diagonals likewise are strengthened and are less likely to lose character in reproduction.

Method of reproduction must also be considered in the choice and application of type styles and the paper surface must be taken into consideration also. Offset and gravure, because they are photographic processes, test the serviceability of various type styles more, in certain instances, than does the letterpress method of printing.

The choice of Bodoni to print on a highly coated or smooth-surfaced paper, upon which all of the type's fine characteristics will be evident, is good practice. Use of this type on rough antique stock that requires undue impression and an abundance of ink changes its character and handicaps its expressiveness.

An Old Style type whose ultimate design value is expressed when letterpress printed on deckle edge antique stock, obviously is a correct choice. When in doubt, a good compromise can often be effected with a Transitional style which is adaptable to a wide variety of paper and reproduction processes.

Beginning of Sans Serif Era

It is a coincidence that both the original type style (Gothic Text) which is characterized by elaborate decorative embellishments, and its extreme opposite, the Sans Serif style which typifies extreme unadorned simplicity, should be of German origin.

Their structures are widely separated in skeletal form and surface treatment. Use of Gothic Text is very limited in contemporary layout practice while the Sans Serif style is used predominantly in display in both advertising and printing typography.

The Sans Serif style, being the same skeletal form as the Old Style, Transitional and Modern, likewise traces its origin to the classic Roman inscriptions on stone of early centuries but it differs in surface style. Being devoid of all serifs and maintaining a uniformity of weight in the curvilinear and angular strokes, which are directly traceable

to the rule and compass of the draftsman, the Sans Serif style, as best typified by Futura, the most famous in its class, requires a separate classification and different techniques for its application in layout and typography.

Forerunner of the Sans Serif importations of the 1920s was the Kabel series which was surpassed in popularity in 1928 by the creation of Paul Renner's Futura in Munich. This skeletonized Roman type from which all unessentials had been eliminated fit so definitely into the ever expanding field of contemporary design that its versatility has since been recognized. It has been emulated, redesigned and adapted to every form of type casting and typesetting technique.

The appropriateness of the Sans Serif types to layout patterns which include such contemporary applications as bleed halftones, expansive areas of color, reverse plates and surprints of type and illustration on a wide variety of screen tints is quite evident when one examines the typography of the smarter magazines of today. Likewise its wide use in direct mail and other creative printing is quite obvious. The Futura sheet from the Eastern Corp. series quite graphically illustrates how the utter simplicity of the types is characterized and accentuated by the harmony of the layout pattern which likewise is functionally sound but simple and unadorned.

Because of its emphatic quality, high visability and broadness of color range the Sans Serif style can express many moods, accentuate definite atmosphere and give structural strength and ruggedness in varying degrees of tone.

The Sans Serif Style, properly chosen for body weight, correctly letterspaced, wordspaced and intelligently leaded, adds sparkle in endless variety. Sans

Serif can be as feminine as a lipstick or as rugged as a battleship. Its structural and tone variances are adaptable to both formal and informal layouts but it disports itself with greater freedom and expressiveness in layouts that stem from informality and subtle proportioning and patterning of highly contrasting elements in expansive areas of white space.

While highly adaptable to many forms of display headings, subheads and limited amounts of text, it becomes monotonous if set too lengthily, in the smaller sizes particularly.

The tendency to "over display" by the over use of Sans Serifs types can be modified by combining them as display elements with text set in some well selected Modern or Transitional face.

The term "Gothic," as it relates to the stiff mechanical faces such as Alternate Gothic, Franklin Gothic, News Gothic and others whose directness of line and absence of serif quite properly associates them with the Sans Serif types, is a designation that stems from their comparison years ago with Gothic Text forms in blackness of body. Constant repetition by type founders and printers of the term "Gothic" has caused these types to be known as such. However any similarity can be dispelled by adding the term "Text" when the decorative form is specified.

The popularity of the above named types and others in the "Gothic" category is due to the great versatility of these types, some wider, some narrower, some heavier, some lighter.

Because of their more rigid vertical effect than most Sans Serif types the Gothics are favored for building narrow, strong vertical patterns such as in single column layouts, or where a hard-hitting display line is required in limited width. Obviously the condensed versions of the Sans Serifs are likewise utilized. Expanded Gothics are also available in many weights.

Letterspacing of the condensed types should not be overdone as the obvious character of the letter form tends to compactness. However, an occasional line, letterspaced to achieve a definite width for design purposes is refreshing.

Square Serifs Are Structural

Square Serif faces are not new, the style having originated in France over a century ago. Their use in America is traceable to the great variety of handbill printing of years ago. The "reincarnation" of this type form, however, awaited the refinements in such splendid designs as Girder, Beton, Stymie, Cairo, Memphis, Rockwell and others.

The term "Square Serif" stems from the mechanical form which is accentuated by the rigid, right-angular serif

of the same weight as the body. Beton like Futura in the San Serifs, has utmost variation in weight from light to extra bold, all of which are recommended for building strong structural patterns. Most weights are mainly monotone in character but the extra bold versions of Square Serifs have a slight thinning of serifs and crossbars.

The text sizes are round and easy to read but their choice must be predicated on suitable copy theme and layout objective, otherwise they may bring undue structural and tone weight to the typography. In short they are not "bookish" in character.

The Contemporary Types

Types of Contemporary origin such as Lydian, Cartoon, Flash and the Modern Script varieties like Brush, Kaufman, Gillies Gothic and Signal have their own individuality and distinction and to avoid endless style classifications are grouped together. As each requires particular treatment depending mainly on the copy theme and typographic objective, we refrain from any general observations on usage of these types.

We have selected the ATFs' Grayda to illustrate, in the accompanying Eastern reproduction, how extreme and unrelated to the classical Roman structure are some of the Contemporary types.

1803	1947
L'ÉCRITURE des Egyptiens 1234567890	STYMIE Light
L'ÉTUDE comparative	STYMIE Light Italic
UNE EXPOSITION Concours Amusants	STYMIE Medium
TECHNIQUES de Laboratoire	STYMIE Medium Italic
ARME Latine	STYMIE Bold
MERLE	STYMIE Bold Italic
CANTON	STYMIE Extra Bold
LES DÉPUTÉS DU 4 JUILLET	STYMIE Extra Bold Italic
LES ARMES Egyptiennes 1234567890	STYMIE Extra Bold Condensed
Les Directions AÉRIENNES	STYMIE Extra Bold Condensed Italic
TRAVAUX artistiques	STYMIE BOLD OPEN
DANS L'ÉGYPTE ANTIQUE Homère, Eschyle, Socrate	GOLD RUSH
CARNOT, LOUBET Marché Constantin	ANTIQUE SHADED
POILU Ancien	FRAMED EGYPTIAN
Molière	EGYPTIAN CONDENSED
LEGENDE Farfadets.5	CRADIENT AL LETTER
RALYE	
MONLOT PENOLAN	
DÉSILENETS DUC BERRI	
LAURIE NEHAR	
DUBOLE	
SUCRE	
GANDVIE RBUSTA	
ANOUE	
GEOFFROY HILAIRE FEUILLE AUTOMNE MUSIQUE AIR	

The informal advertisement above was reproduced in line direct from a newspaper tear sheet. In this instance all type was set by the newspaper in a sans serif style combined with Bodoni. The rugged masculinity of the type is carried through both logotypes at the top of the ad.

The rugged structural qualities of the Square-Serif types is exemplified in the Eastern sheet at the right. The "window-frame" pattern forms a symmetrical structure with obvious panels for type enclosures.

THIS IS A SPECIMEN SHEET OF SQUARE-SERIF

MANIFEST BOND is a crisp, clean, economical paper that runs smoothly on the press . . . a true performer that takes good printing easily and quickly. Firm, uniform surfaces . . . free from waves, wrinkles and troublesome lint . . . precision trimmed edges and a sturdy texture insure cleaner, sharper impressions with a minimum of waste, stoppages and other troubles that cost a printer time and money.

THIS IS A SPECIMEN SHEET OF EASTERN'S MANIFEST BOND

EASTERN CORPORATION · · BANGOR, MAINE
Makers of ATLANTIC BOND and Other Fine Business Papers

The above enlargement of the side panels of the Eastern sheet at the left quite graphically reiterate that "there is nothing new under the Sun" in basic type design.

GOTHIC TEXT

𝕲𝖔𝖚𝖉𝖞 𝕿𝖊𝖝𝖙   𝕮𝖑𝖔𝖎𝖘𝖙𝖊𝖗 𝕭𝖑𝖆𝖈𝖐   𝕺𝖑𝖉 𝕰𝖓𝖌𝖑𝖎𝖘𝖍

OLD STYLE

Caslon   Garamond   Goudy

MODERN

Bodoni   Mondial   **Onyx**

TRANSITIONAL

Bulmer   Scotch Roman   Baskerville

SQUARE SERIF

Stymie   Beton   Girder

SANS SERIF

Futura   Kabel   **Bernhard Gothic**

SCRIPT

Typo Script   *Bond Script*   *Trafton Script*

CURSIVE

Bernhard Cursive   *Coronet*   *Mozart*

CONTEMPORARY

Eve   **Lydian**   CARTOON

146

The War Messages of Franklin D. Roosevelt

SUPPLEMENT: NOVEMBER 7, 1942 TO JULY 20, 1943

The President's War Addresses to the People of the United States, to the Congress of the United States, and to Other Nations

Title page of a historical document set in Bulmer.

Proper Planning for Readability

Proper Planning for *Readability*

PROPER *Planning* FOR READABILITY

Proper Planning *for* READABILITY

Proper Planning for Readability

PROPER PLANNING FOR *Readability*

Proper Planning for
Readability

Proper
Planning for Readability

PROPER PLANNING
for Readability

Proper Planning
for READABILITY

Proper
Planning
for Readability

PROPER
PLANNING
FOR *Readability*

Proper
Planning
for READABILITY

Muskrat makes campus news

For that sparkling-fresh, young look!

EXCITING! ENTICING! IT'S SPICED CINNAMON

a great car for YOU, too!

inspiration for your holiday

TOYS in the 1948 shops

Ruffle of Excitement!

what everybody wants...

PUNCTUATION WITH A *Punch*

reductions of 25% and 50%

you'll be walking on air

This is the *Ultimate*

THE WORLD is out of Balance!

Norwegian Blue Fox Jackets

Repeat success!

The marvelous nylon socks that stood New York on its ear!

An outstanding value at 1.00

Wednesday at 8 a.m.

Various forms of emphasis in headings and other units of display type are shown in these reductions from newspapers and magazines.

Proper Planning
for
Readability

Examples in left column show how various degrees of display emphasis may be obtained by utilizing the various letter forms available in a single type style. Top examples are one-line settings in Caslon Oldstyle, employing roman caps and lower case; italic caps and lower case, and small caps.

LAYOUT IS AN ART
Layout is an Art
Layout is an Art
LAYOUT IS AN ART
LAYOUT IS AN ART
Layout is an Art
Layout is an Art
Layout is an Art
Layout is an Art
Layout is an Art
Layout is an Art
Layout is an Art
Layout is an Art
Layout is an Art

Each line above is set entirely in one size and style of type. Below are some experimental settings which combine various forms and styles to evaluate display emphasis. The first four lines are set in varying forms of the same type style. The last four combine different styles as well as forms.

LAYOUT is an Art
LAYOUT *is an Art*
Layout IS AN ART
Layout *is an Art*

Layout is an Art
Layout *is an Art*
Layout is an Art
Layout *is an Art*

Middle examples are two-line arrangements which show Garamond Oldstyle in varying forms of display emphasis and differently proportioned line widths. The settings are formal or symmetrically balanced.

Bottom left examples utilize Bodoni Book, a Modern type classification, set in three variations of the flush left arrangement. This style of setting typifies much of the display in informal or assymmetrically balanced layouts.

The three-line formal arrangement at immediate left employs Bulmer, a "transitional" face which is ideally suited for either symmetrical or non-symmetrical layouts.

Fitting Copy to Text Areas

HAVING ESTABLISHED approximate areas for text masses on a layout, it is essential that the copy for each area be computed to fit into its dimensions in the proper type size and with the correct leading.

The most generally used method for fitting typewritten copy to text areas is that which reduces the manuscript copy to a definite number of lines of a particular type size according to the amount of type characters in the width of the line. The amount of type lines multiplied by the type height in points gives the minimum depth in points needed for the copy. This depth may then be increased by leading between the type lines.

Having selected a style and size of type, refer to a specimen book to ascertain the number of type characters that will fit in the pica width of the text mass on the layout.

On the first line of the manuscript copy place a small pencil mark at the required number of typewriter characters necessary to fill a type line. Draw a vertical line from this point downward on the manuscript. Count the number of lines to the left of the vertical line. Convert the total of all odd characters at the right of the vertical line into type lines by counting all characters and dividing by the line character count. Add both counts and this will give the total number of type lines the copy will make. Cast each paragraph separately and count each space as a character.

In estimating previously printed copy for resetting, count several average lines for character count and multiply this by the total number of lines. This gives the total character count.

Dividing the number of type characters in the new line width into the total of characters in the printed copy will give the approximate number of new type lines the copy will make.

It is obvious that various styles and sizes of type have varying character counts in a line of specified width. To facilitate copy fitting calculations the layout man should use one of the reference charts that list the average character count of the most widely used types in varying widths.

149

Type specimen books which show foundry faces and slug-casting machine types should always be handy for ready reference.

For those who are inexperienced in type measurements, it may be explained that there are 72 points to the inch. The height of type is always specified in points. If the type is of 8 point body there are nine lines of type to the inch. In 12 point type there are six lines to the inch, and so on. Adding one, two or more points of leading between lines obviously increases the amount of space type occupies in depth.

There are 12 points to a pica; six picas to an inch. All typesetting instructions should be given in these terms which are used by all printers.

In approximating the amount of words necessary to fill a certain text area, the following procedure is suggested: ascertain how many type characters there are in a line of the selected type and multiply by the number of lines necessary to fill the area. This will give the total number of characters, which divided by six (characters in the average word) will give the number of words necessary to fill the area.

This type is 6 pt. Bodoni, set 28½ picas wide, solid. The measure is too wide for a continuous reading of the text, since the eye cannot comfortably follow repeated lines set in this width. This size type should be set in approximately the following measure:

This is 6 pt. Bodoni type, same as above, set 12 picas or one and three-fourth times its alphabet length.

This is 8 pt. Bodoni, set solid, 28½ picas wide and again the measure is much too wide for the eye to easily follow the text. This size type should be set about 16 picas wide as shown below:

This is 8 pt. Bodoni type, same as above, set one and three-fourths times its alphabet length in points.

This is 10 pt. Bodoni, set solid, 28½ picas wide, which even for this size type is still too wide a measure for comfortable reading. Below is a better width.

So, here is 10 pt. Bodoni, set in 19-pica width, or one and three-fourths its alphabet length.

This is 12 pt. Bodoni type, set 28½ picas wide, a measure that still is too wide for easy readability. A better line width is seen below:

A better width for a line of 12 pt. Bodoni is this 21-pica measure, following the rule explained above.

Achieving Effects with Typographical Material

OCCASIONALLY THE LAYOUT MAN must attain quickly an unusual effect and is limited in time and expense for art work and plates; or perhaps he may evolve an idea that can be interpreted best by some novel typographical treatment. He then avails himself of the practically unlimited typographical facilities in the composing room, such as rules, dingbats, borders, ornaments, tint blocks, and other typographical accessories and creates from them effects that are unique and practical.

The typographical equipment of the modern composing room offers unlimited inspiration to the versatile layout man, and the ever-increasing supply of new fonts and accessories makes possible apparently unlimited effects.

With a fertile imagination and a thorough understanding of mechanical procedures and limitations, the layout man can create novel layouts that any competent compositor can interpret.

Some of the techniques are: combining type characters and ornaments in decorative shapes and illustrative forms; employing rules to form entire letters, parts of letters or decorative shadings; combining ornamental spots with rules or parts of letters to simulate decorative objects; trimming plates or blocks to unusual shapes, printing them in color and overprinting them with type or accessories.

151

★ ★ ★ ★ ★ ★ ★ ★ ★ ★

"IT'S GOT TO REACH
THE **L**EADERS IN EVERY
INCOME GROUP..."

Okay...it's a tough ticket!

Now...let's see how one magazine measures up...

"*I want my advertising where people spend time reading it!*"

THE **G**REAT NAMES
IN ADVERTISING

"**I**T'S GOT TO REACH
A WHALE OF A LOT OF READERS
...where my products are sold"

Five examples of type headings with harmonious rule, ornament and initial combinations that were set "right out of the case." In the top left example the initial is an open face letter with the stars imprinted separately.

Top right example utilizes thick and thin rectangular rule combination with the Modern type style. Ultra Bodoni Italic. The right center proof shows how the curved thick and thin characteristics of Gloria type are accentuated by a gradation of various rule thicknesses combined with a curved, tapering rule.

The frivolous ornamentation in the bottom left example typifies the decorative style that was prevalent when Gold Rush type was popular.

The initial in the bottom right proof was composed of rules in a manner that accentuates the shaded Greco Adornado type.

"**W**hat
weekly magazine would you prefer for the **ADVERTISING** of the products you handle?"

2,000 Lumber Dealers were questioned. 37.0% who answered named the POST. 4¼ times as many as for the next highest magazine.)

2,000 Paint Dealers were questioned. 24.4% who answered named the POST. (Almost half again as much as the next highest magazine.)

When 18,677 customers of leading Men's Wear stores across the country were asked: "In what weekly magazine do you pay the most attention to advertising?" 45% who answered named the POST. (More than the next two highest magazines combined.)

291 Automotive Dealers and Parts Wholesalers were questioned. 59.3% who answered named the POST. (Over twice as many as for the next highest magazine.)

500 Bearing Distributors were questioned. 35.1% who answered named the POST. (Nearly 4 times as many as for the next highest magazine.)

1,050 Automotive Parts and Accessories Distributors were questioned. 44.2% who answered named the POST. (Almost half again as much as the next highest magazine.)

The text masses in this typographical presentation are unified by the vertical bracket. This entire element is then unified optically with the side head by the horizontal decorative border.

Even the illustrations were set "right out of the case" in this all type, rule and dingbat composition at the right.

Advertising

IMPACT

TINY TRAIN AD HAS TREMENDOUS PULL

▶ "Our advertisement actually put us into a business which we never contemplated entering—the mail order business." It was only a 28-line ad—yet the results were astounding. The advertisement described and pictured two miniature plastic trains made by Hensy Toys. It only made three appearances in The Saturday Evening Post last year. Despite its small size, the ad pulled many hundreds of orders and letters from all over the United States and a dozen foreign countries.

The Art of Selling Books

● When Watson-Guptill Publications, Inc., planned their advertising campaign for "Norman Rockwell, Illustrator," they included a quarter-page in the Post. They expected that Post readers would show considerable interest in the book, but they weren't prepared for the record-breaking number of orders—at $10 per book—they received. The publishers estimate that this one ad sold between $35,000 and $45,000 worth of books in three months. Cost of ad: $2500.

HOW LONG DO POST ADS LIVE?

☆ They live on and on and on. A recent example, for instance, is a letter received a while ago by Stromberg-Carlson in which the writer enclosed a coupon for a booklet on radio sets. The ad appeared back in 1940. And as another example of long life (and not too rare), the Greenfield Tap and Die Corporation recently got a request for their Repair Tool Booklet offered in an ad that appeared in an issue of the Post published (no foolin') 'way back in 1917.

Meat Spread Spreads Out!

Advertisers will find a lot of meat in this story: In April, 1946 the Smithfield Ham & Products Co., Inc., decided to tell Post readers about delicious James River Deviled Smithfield Meat Spread. They ran quarter pages every other week—and merchandised them to the hilt with special Saturday Evening Post reprint cards, folders, and booklets. By July—hold your breath—they checked in one important area and found business was up 600%!

does anyone read ads this small?

Cedar Laboratories, makers of Seal-Skin Hand Cream, ran a 21-line ad like this in the Post. They were angling for new dealers and, we're happy to report, got 100 inquiries, plus $3,000 in orders. Great little trade magazine, the Post!

And we could show you volumes on the same subject— every one an eye-opener! BUT, AS FINAL PROOF...

To be completely effective, each typographical element must be chosen with careful regard for its optical influence and every detail of composition planned with precision.

Layouts of this type need not be meticulous from an artistic standpoint, but they must be essentially practical. A simple rough on tracing paper will suffice if it conveys the idea to the compositor and is based on a practical understanding of composition and available materials.

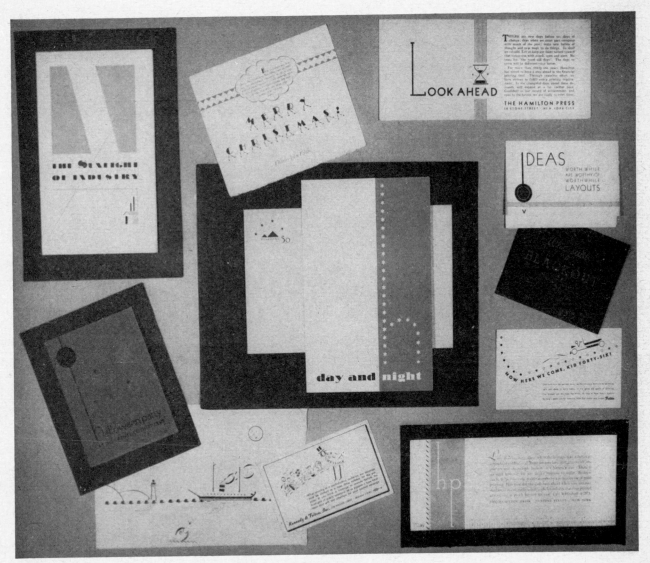

Examples of printed material produced entirely with type, rules, ornaments, typographical accessories, and an occasional tint block or "positive" engraving made from a type proof. Absolutely no art work was employed in the production of this material, composed by the author.

PART EIGHT

Color...Its Effective Application

THE THEORY that there are but *three primary colors*—red, yellow and blue, is the most practical for layout purposes, as the processes of color engraving, ink making and printing are all based on this principle. From these primary colors all other colors are obtained.

The *secondary colors* are green, orange and violet. Orange is a combination of red and yellow; green is a combination of yellow and blue; violet is a combination of red and blue.

The *tertiary colors* are citrine, a combination of orange and green; olive, a combination of green and violet; and russet, a combination of orange and violet.

The various hues may be obtained by combining one neighboring color with another, such as red and orange to achieve red orange, blue and green to obtain blue green, and so on. The color that predominates is known as the dominating hue. By adding black or white to a color a *tone* is achieved; black making it a *shade* and white making it a *tint*.

Colors are said to be complementary to each other when they compose together agreeably. Any color in the primary trio is complementary to a combination of the other two colors. For example, red is complementary to green which is a combination of yellow and blue; yellow is complementary to violet, which is a combination of red and blue; blue is complementary to orange, which is a combination of red and yellow. This theory applies, likewise, to the secondary and tertiary groups.

Colors are classified as "warm" and "cold" on the theory that their optical influences create physical reactions. The warm colors are red, yellow, orange, yellow green, and any combinations which they dominate. These colors, by their association with the sun, fire and other warm elements of

154

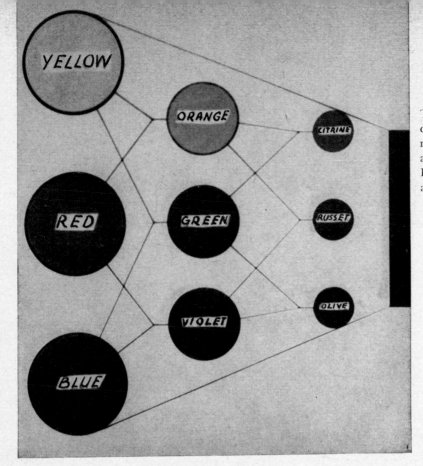

This chart illustrates the basic principles of the use of the three primary colors, yellow, red and blue and the colors evolving from them. Black results from a combination of all colors.

nature, convey to our minds the physical properties of these objects. Likewise the cold colors, such as blue, violet, green, and any combinations which they dominate, suggest the coolness of the sea, the sky and other elements. The pale tints of the warm colors have long been associated with feminine tastes, while the cooler colors are said to be masculine.

Black is not a color but is a combination of all colors. Black, gray, gold and silver, harmonize or contrast with any color. Pure gray has a neutral effect, but can be warmed with yellow or cooled with blue or black.

Guided by these basic fundamentals, the layout man, by constant experiments, intuition and good taste, should develop a keen color sense and appreciation for color harmony and contrast. Restraint should be used and simple color combinations only be attempted by the layout beginner.

The pure primary colors, red, yellow and blue, are strong, blatant colors, and should be used sparingly. They should only be used when sharp attention value and utmost contrast is wanted. Tints and shades of primary colors and the secondary colors are more pleasing for most layout purposes.

By adding black to a color a darker shade is obtained.

By adding white to a color a lighter tint is obtained.

For utmost color harmony it is advisable to use simple combinations of hues, such as dark and light blue, dark and light green, and so on. Dazzling areas of incorrect color distract the eye and lessen attention value.

Introduction of intermediate tones, tints, neutral gray or black, in the proper proportion, gives a composition variety and sparkle.

Color must be positioned skillfully for balance. A warm-colored initial, placed against a cool type mass, balances the composition, but if it is overshadowed by large areas of cold color, its value is lost. Likewise if all color is in one part of a layout it is unbalanced. Its proper distribution cannot be fixed by rule but rather accomplished by good taste and the ingenuity of the designer.

The color of paper stock, its relationship to various colors and their printability thereon must be considered carefully, as effects that are painted readily with opaque water colors or sketched with crayons are not always as easily attained with printing inks. When in doubt, the layout man should consult the pressman on the printing of unusual color combinations.

Constant experimentation with color mixing, ink and paper combinations, and the acquisition of a store of workable techniques is the most practical way of mastering color application.

Below are eight color patterns which create three-dimensional effects by control of color tonal values in widely different ways. Variation in size, shape, tone and position is underlying procedure while actual perspective in drawing is obvious in several examples.

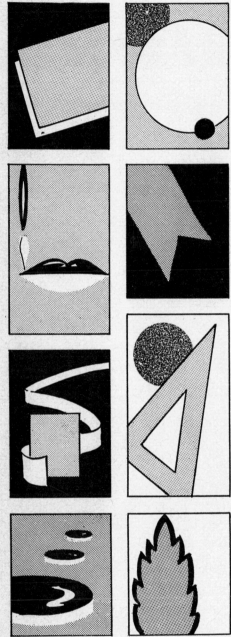

All of the extreme left examples in the four horizontal rows of basic color patterns in upper right panel illustrate the static appearance of layouts that divide space too mechanically. In the top left, the widths of the vertical color bands are identical to the vertical white space between them. This divides the layout width into three mathematically alike vertical areas. The circular element, by being centrally placed in the vertical area, creates top and bottom space margins that are alike. Both left and right extremities of the circular element divide each color band exactly in half.

In the next two improved examples to the right, the same size circular element is positioned vertically so as to achieve unequal top and bottom margins. In the first revision, the widths of the color bands are reduced so that, while a symmetrical pattern is maintained, variety is attained by the non-mathematical variance of these two vertical bands to the center white vertical band. The circle does not now halve the vertical color bands.

The second revision (third top example) creates an informally balanced pattern wherein further liberties are taken with the widths of the vertical color bands, which now have greater contrast to the white vertical band.

The extreme right top layout increases the size of the circular element and shifts its position to evaluate another type of informal balance. The vertical color bands likewise are varied. The width extremities of the circular element also are non-measurable optically in relation to the widths of the color bands.

In the other three horizontal rows, the three redesigned patterns in each instance make the color pattern more interesting by applying the principle of *proportion* in the sizing and shaping of color units.

Right—The four thumbnails show (1) how a large area of black is "warmed" by a proportionate amount of color (gray tone); (2) a large area of color is contrasted to a large black head and a black lower right illustration; (3) approximately the same technique as in (2) but the white vertical area gives a third value to relieve the black horizontal panel; (4) a vertical black band relieved by a horizontal color element.

The bottom panels show (1) how black outlines will give necessary emphasis to a light-color initial; (2) an italic decorative initial in black "cooling" a "warm" color area; (3) an emphatic color initial at top left of the layout counterbalances the elements at the right.

Expanding Color Patterns

In these days of continually rising costs in every phase of Graphic Arts production, the question of how we can get more mileage from our creative endeavors should prompt every printing planner to evaluate the utmost potentials in every basic layout idea and design.

The possibilities for expanding layout patterns are practically endless (particularly when a second color is employed), limited only by the imagination and ingenuity of the designer.

For example: once a two-color pattern has been utilized wherein the color is a dominant structural design, it is often possible to redesign other quite different layouts by utilizing the original color pattern and creating entirely new elements to accompany it in the black pattern.

On the succeeding pages, we experiment with the four basic color patterns shown vertically on the previous page, and by varying the size, shape, tone and position of the illustrative and typographical elements that combine with the basic color pattern, while retaining the fundamental color structure, some novel and interesting thumbnails result.

In each horizontal row of layouts on the following pages, gradations of tone, surprints, reverses and other photo-mechanical techniques are shown.

158

Right—The first row shows a symmetrically balanced pattern activated by variations of style in headline display, change of widths in textual and illustrative elements and regulation of tonal values to achieve varying forms of emphasis.

The second row of informally balanced thumbnails allocates in each instance a more diversified number of layout elements to the geometric horizontal and vertical rule pattern which divides each layout.

In the first thumbnail, the large area at the left of the dominant vertical color band provides ample space for displaying the heading and the main text arranged in an axis type of format which quickly leads the eye down to the trade-mark. The two horizontal color rules subtly separate the main text from the textual element at the top and the logotype at the bottom. The extreme right vertical element could be a panel of type of some subordinate copy or, likewise, an illustration. This "organization" of copy stems from a thorough analysis of the relative importance of all typographical and pictorial elements from the standpoint of design.

The second sketch utilizes the skeletonized color pattern in a definitely contrasting manner. The pictorial element, vaguely suggested at the top left, receives dominant display by such placement, and because of shape and tone.

The other two examples in this row and in the two rows below further illustrate the possibilities of adapting a basic color pattern to a wide variety of layout ideas.

The four examples below are achieved by reversing the basic color patterns shown above and by applying to them a variety of harmonizing black patterns. This illustrates how "more mileage" may be obtained from basic art work by the simple expedient of making a "positive" engraving, offset or gravure plate.

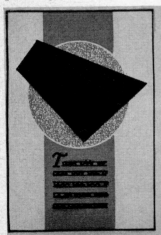

unifying element in a more "airy" and informal style of layout.

The third sketch is a more commercial adaptation of the color pattern, the vertical of which here acts to emphasize the main illustrative element at the bottom right, whose tone value is strengthened in relation to the similarly shaped elements which fade in perspective to the top left of the layout. Here the weight of the head and the signature at bottom left help equalize optical balance. The fourth sketch is a semi-humorous adaptation, wherein the large curvilinear element at the left is counterbalanced by the logotype at top right. The vertical color band unifies this element with the left foreground element.

The deep vertical design feeling in the first thumbnail in the third row is accentuated by containing all black elements in the white panel at left and creating rhythm by the placement of the symbolic foreign language elements in reverse on the vertical color area down the right of the layout.

In contrast is the broader feel existing in the second thumbnail which dominantly displays the rectangular element at the top. The larger "d" in display, together with the eye-attraction of the signature in reverse at the bottom, helps equalize balance.

In the third sketch, weight of black elements may be said to predominate at the right, but the size and style of the "S" in signature compensates commensurably.

The large head in the fourth sketch in the top left dominant position compensates for the weight of the main illustration and the "product" displayed at the bottom right.

In the bottom row, the first is a purely typographical interpretation wherein the extreme emphasis of weight of elements at right could be relieved by toning the values of both right black and color values.

In the second sketch, the weight of the black lower left element compensates for the lighter tonal values of both the color and black elements at the right. The reverse head at top right of the color panel in the third sketch is counterbalanced by the angular placement of the illustrative element at bottom left. The final sketch evaluates a less commercial type of layout which utilizes a variation of color tones to create interest and form a decorative unifying element for the illustration of the woman's head.

Above—The first example in the top row places a purely typographical heading in a circular mortise on the basic color background in which the small reverse logotype at the bottom, left of the suggested signature, is the only departure from the original color pattern. In the second, the heading at bottom right is reversed in the color pattern to give added variety and subordination to the dominant rectangular black display element at the top which is drawn in perspective to increase the tri-dimensional effect and provide the layout with "depth."

The third thumbnail places the illustrative element in a different form of perspective at the bottom of the layout, with the base at eye-level. The smaller, yet forceful, heading, by its placement in the circular white panel, receives ample prominence. The heading in the fourth is much more subordinated than in the previous sketches, both by reduction in size and through its relegation and reversal in the top right color background. In the first sketch of the second row, the black heading style and the light-toned illustration underneath are counterbalanced by the deep vertical color band at the right.

The vertical, irregularly outlined elements in the right margin suggest type elements of lesser importance.

The second thumbnail suggests how the basic color pattern can be utilized as a

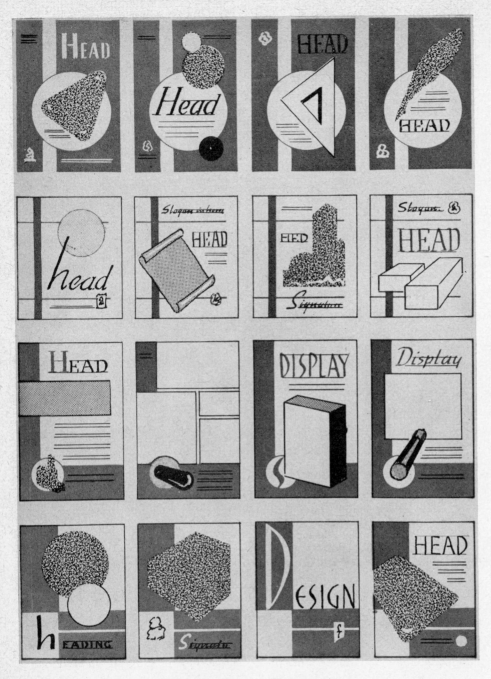

ment accentuates the dominantly vertical pattern, but an effort is made to introduce subtle contrast by suggesting some angular and semi-circular contours in the illustrative element. The fourth sketch introduces perspective by the shapes of the two illustrative elements at the bottom of the layout. In each of the four layouts in this row a varying degree of emphasis will be noted in the size and style of the heading.

The first example in the third row introduces a sharply contrasting horizontal pictorial element at the top left of the thumbnail, creating interest by variety of shapes. The initial in the lower circular mortise is well coordinated with the shape of the opening, while in the next sketch the same circular mortise acts as a contrasting shape to the illustrative element which by its directional quality points to the last line at the bottom. The third example again, by its dominantly vertical illustration, emphasizes the depth of the layout area which, while the same as others in the row, appears to be more vertical because of its continuing vertical lines. The last sketch in this row utilizes a rectangular, horizontal shape in high center position to divide the area more interestingly.

The two circular elements in the first sketch in the bottom row dominate the layout forcefully in logical sequence, the vertical color band at the left accentuating the top one and the top horizontal band the bottom one. Balance is maintained by emphasizing the "h" initial at bottom left.

The perspective angularity of the dominant element in the second sketch effectively contrasts with the vertical and horizontal shapes of the color bands. Here the dominant typographical element is the subordinated signature in the bottom horizontal which, while subordinate, gets sufficient emphasis because of the directional qualities in the illustration direct attention to it subtly.

In the third sketch, the color bands act only as emphasis and coordinating elements to frame the initial letter and the logo, allowing white space, by contrast, to add distinction and freedom.

The last example is an extreme variation of the "cut-in" technique and, by contrast with its left neighbor, shows how uniformly harmonious or blatantly contrasting a manner one may elaborate on a basic color pattern.

Above—All of the thumbnails shown are informally balanced. The top left example gives dominance to the pictorial element displayed in the circular mortise of the color pattern while giving the head ample display emphasis at the top right. Reversing the head on color adds depth to the pattern. In the next example, the heading receives emphatic display in the circular mortise and the three remaining circular elements are effectively subordinated in display value, but subtly placed in rhythmic progression and thereby unified effectively. In the third example, the heading is subordinated and the sharp angular contrast of the illustrative element placed against the circular element again gives the illustrative

element extreme emphasis. The fourth thumbnail uses the qualities in the illustrative element to bring attention to the less dominant heading.

The first sketch in the second horizontal row utilizes the top horizontal color band as a unifying element between the dominant circular element at top right and the vertical color band at extreme left, then the bottom horizontal band unifies the vertical with the logotype at bottom right. In the second example, the vertical color bar is sharply contrasted to the angular scroll-like element at lower left, which is unified much like the previous example with the lower right logotype. In the third example, the vertical shape of the illustrative ele-

Applying Depth and Perspective with Color

The attainment of depth and perspective with color need not be predicated on costly art work and elaborate photoengraving, offset or gravure processes, but may consist only of some simple design device that results from proper cropping, silhouetting, mortising, grouping or placement of a simple color screen tint panel, pictorial element in line or halftone, or other decorative device. Depth and perspective may also be accomplished by utilizing simple typographical devices such as rules, brackets, dingbats and other accessories used in proper association with type and other very practical design elements.

Likewise, in limited editions of letterpress printing, the utilization of rubber, plastic and other tint plates is economical and practical.

Right—First example in the thumbnails illustrates the basic step in giving a rectangular rule panel the illusion of depth, by the addition of color shadow rules at bottom and right. The top center rough reverses the shadow angle to bottom and left. The top right example adds still another plane and a color shadow behind the circular element.

The second below top left example places a simple, initial "T" over a circular color tint at an angle that gives an illusion of depth.

The next to right grouping is but one of many possible variations of coupon grouping. Here it is interestingly unified by placement over a circular color panel and under the arrow-shaped color panel. The extreme right sketch also effectively unifies three differently shaped elements. The left center layout creates interest by contrasting the color shadowed diagonal panel on a toned background.

In the dead center example, the horizontal rule which connects the male figure with the emblem under the signature creates the illusion of depth as does the panel in the fore of the figure. The "Heading" arrangement to the right attains depth by overlapping of elements of contrasting size, shape and tone. Occasionally type overprints on phantom-like or simply outlined color elements may effectively be employed as in the "Heading across" example.

All three of the pictorial type of layouts at bottom left employ a variation of the mortised panel technique for creating depth.

The bottom center rough employs a simpler, more horizontally patterned pictorial element which emphasizes the mortised panel effectively.

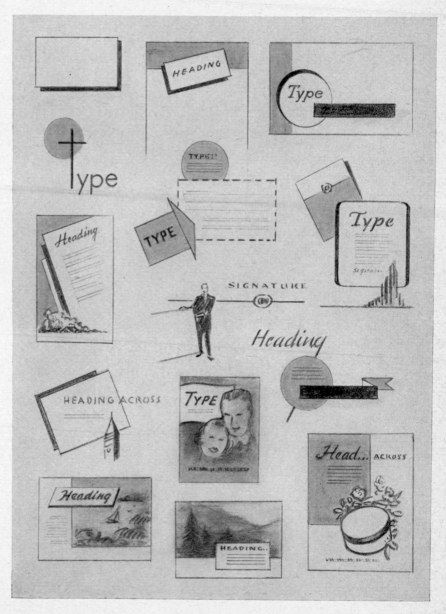

Selecting Paper Stock

THE ADVERTISING of a leading paper manufacturer stresses the wide influence paper stock exerts in making printing effective, by its slogan—"Paper is part of the picture."

Paper stock is indeed, one of the most important assets of the printing planner, if its utmost possibilities are fully utilized.

Distinctive typography, characterful photographs and art work, good plates, the proper ink and the finest presswork are essential to the correct interpretation of any layout; but they will not be efficiently coordinated unless the proper paper is used.

Paper stocks are available in such a wide variety of colors, finishes, weights and sizes as to make them adaptable to an unlimited variety of layout techniques and fullest advantage should be taken of these elements in the preliminary planning stages.

In newspaper and magazine printing, practicability demands a uniform paper stock that is most adaptable to the particular reproductive technique of each individual publication. Broadsides, folders, booklets, brochures, announcements, stationery and other commercial printing, however, offer the versatile layout man wide latitude in specifying color and texture in paper stock. Here he can find expression for individuality and imagination.

The experienced layout man avoids specifying weird and unrelated color combinations of paper and ink, relying on white, or the softer pastel shades of stock, printed in harmonious colors.

Paper manufacturers have done much research in color harmony. The many color combinations advocated in their sample books and promotional material are the result of much experiment and can be successfully followed by the layout man.

There are papers to suit every purpose. Appropriateness, due regard for cost, and practicability should govern the choice. An all rag content paper should be specified if the printing is to be of a permanent nature, while a sulphite or other less costly stock will suffice if the job is to have limited usage. Some types of stock lend themselves well to gumming, varnishing, die cutting, embossing and other finishing while others do not. All other mechanical limitations, likewise, must be evaluated in order to secure the utmost in reproduction.

A layout that contains type alone can be interpreted on a wide range of antique stocks, while one with halftones or other fine details must be printed on a coated paper or a highly supercalendered stock if printed by letterpress. When paper cost, mailing weight, or mechanical limitations are factors, the choice may be an English finish. For strict economy, a job may be printed on newsprint, provided cuts are of the proper screen.

The layout man should have a basic knowledge of paper making and if possible he should visit a paper mill to learn paper making at first hand.

It is needless to list the endless variety of paper stocks, as the layout man can secure samples from a local supply house.

While many types of paper are rugged and strong, it is highly sensitive to many presswork procedures. Paper is greatly affected by atmospheric changes and will shrink or stretch, curl and wrinkle on occasion. These and other propensities are thoroughly understood by pressroom experts and their advice will often forestall undue mechanical difficulties.

All paper is made with a grain, resulting from the direction in which the long fibers lay on the paper machine. Paper folds better with the grain than against it, and a booklet or pamphlet should always have the paper grain run vertically, or with the binding edge. Similarly, labels, display cards and other printing should be designed to utilize the "way of the grain" to best advantage.

Uncoated paper has two distinct sides, the "wire side" and the "felt side." The "wire side" is caused by the wire screen of the paper machine and is most pronounced on cover and laid stocks. The character and texture of the stock shows to better advantage if printed on the "felt side."

Embossing and fancy finishes are often applied to certain types of paper at the mill. Printing of type or line cuts can be done effectively on these stocks but to obviate mechanical difficulty, halftones should be printed on coated stock and pebbled or embossed later.

"Will it cut out of standard sizes of paper stock?" One of the most pertinent factors in the economical, efficient planning of printing.

Deckle edges are available on a limited type of antique stocks and only on certain dimensions. Care should be exercised in planning deckle edges to avoid waste in cutting paper. The layout man should plan from available stock sizes whenever possible to avoid undue waste.

The better grade papers are made in limited sizes and should be specified cautiously. Any sizable offcuts should be saved, as many novel uses can be found for them on small impromptu jobs.

Ample gripper margin should always be allowed on paper. The "gripper edge" is the edge that is fed to the grippers that hold the sheet in printing and upon which register in presswork depends. In planning large solids and bleed cuts, one should allow ample paper margins to forestall slurring, wrinkling and other troubles. In most cases paper grain should be in the direction of the printing cylinder width and not around it, especially in the heavier paper stocks.

Whenever possible, it is advisable to consult the pressman and binder in respect to imposition of pages for printing and folding.

Favored with a layout that respects its limitations and utilizes its utmost possibilities, paper can truly play a great part in the printing picture.

Paper specimen portfolios showing various textures, finishes, weights and colors are very helpful in formulating colorful paper and ink combinations. Catalogs and other reference books, giving sheet sizes, and other useful paper information, should be in every layout man's library.

Marking the Layout and Copy

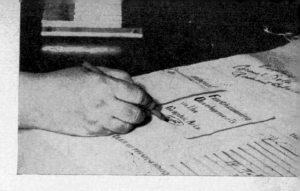

A LAYOUT should be presented for production with typewritten text, photographs, art work and other material properly arranged and explicitly marked to facilitate the mechanics of reproduction.

The typewritten text should be double-spaced with ample margins on letter-size sheets, and numbered in sequence. All display lines should be set off in capitals or otherwise clearly distinguished from text matter. Text areas on the layout should be designated in ringed alphabetical or numerical order and should coincide with identical markings on the typewritten copy. The exact widths and depths of text masses should be clearly marked in pica measures and type sizes and leading specified in points.

In specifying from type catalogs or specimen sheets, the full title of the face and reference number should be given at the outset. Recognizable abbreviations may be used for repeated markings.

Capitals, italics, small caps, indentations, word spacing, letter spacing, ornamentation and other typographic instructions should be marked distinctly on the copy. Colored pencils are recommended for this purpose.

If several mechanical operations are to be done simultaneously, a photostatic copy or rough tracing of the layout should be furnished for each process.

The exact trim size of the finished job should be given in numerals, even though the layout seems obvious.

Instructions for ink matching, presswork, stock size, binding and finishing should be clearly specified.

Photographs should be scaled properly for reduction or enlargement and crop lines marked plainly. Engraving sizes should be requested in pica measurements to facilitate makeup. The screen should be noted as should other essential details such as etching, blocking or retention of bearers for electrotyping moulding.

166

Photographs and other pictorial matter in set-ups or combinations should be marked alphabetically or numerically to conform to the layout. Art work, reproduction proofs, lettering and other engraving copy should be marked clearly for size and covered with a tissue overlay upon which can be shown Ben Day areas, color separations, and other treatments.

It is unwise to rely on verbal instructions in any procedure and the more specific and understandable reproduction instructions are, the more craftsmanlike will be the interpretation.

The materials and techniques available to the designer are practically limitless. Practicability means adapting them to a layout with minimum mechanical effort. Artistic beauty and attractiveness of design are qualities to be desired but they should be coordinated with practicability.

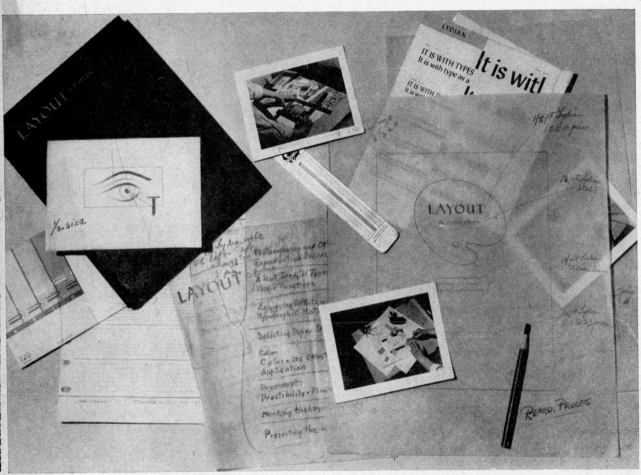

The actual tissue roughs of this volume on which the precise type and engraving specifications were marked. Besides the complete working dummy, some of the actual photographs and art work are discernible in the picture, as are some of the printing planner's essential tools, such as a type gauge, type specimen sheets and samples of engraving screen tints used in this book.

Practicability and Flexibility

"ART FOR ART'S SAKE" is an axiom that should have no place in the lexicon of the layout man. Many layouts defeat their purpose because their designers give vent to artistic obsessions and ignore the major factor in sound printing planning—practicability.

A layout which demands unwarranted mechanical effort makes reproduction complicated and burdensome rather than efficient and helpful. Therefore, layouts which cannot be interpreted without undue cost for art work, typography, plates and presswork should be avoided.

Some of the earmarks of the amateur layout man are: lettering display lines that are too condensed for proper composition in the specified type; crowding subheads into widths and depths that are too contracted for proper type composition; specifying line widths that require excessive letter and word spacing, thereby weakening display value, particularly in lower case; ruling widely miscalculated text areas for specific type sizes; suggesting type arrangements that are freakish and unrelated in shape, size, style and tone; cropping or silhouetting pictures to disproportionate sizes or unpleasant shapes and positioning them in impractical arrangements that require extensive makeup procedures.

Further inconsistencies with practicability are: suggesting freakish ornamentation or combination of unrelated typographic elements, specifying art work and lettering that is tricky, over-ornamented and impractical to reproduce; specifying highly complicated and costly photoengraving techniques; applying lavish, complicated color schemes that require excessive presswork.

The effective advertisements in leading periodicals and outstanding examples of direct mail advertising prove that successful designers understand well the reproductive possibilities and mechanical limitations of graphic presentation. They achieve the utmost in effect with a minimum of effort, both artistically and mechanically.

The attractive and efficient automobile of today far surpasses the one of decades ago in design and construction because from the T-square and drawing board of the modern designer come models that conform to efficient methods of production. Likewise, the design of printing and advertising must conform to the most efficient techniques in reproduction to achieve utmost effectiveness.

Nowhere is the saying "A little knowledge is a dangerous thing" more appropriate than in the planning of printing and advertising. A thorough practical training in the mechanical processes is the best background for efficiency in specifying reproduction procedures. Lacking this training, the layout student should acquire a thorough understanding of all phases of reproduction so that he will avoid elaborate, intricate designs that may satisfy someone's artistic whim, but only confuse the typographer, photoengraver and printer and add needless expense and delay in the mechanical reproduction.

There are no rubber types or elastic plates in a composing room. Copy and its resultant space occupancy in type should be computed with care before drawing definite areas on a layout. Space for halftones and line cuts likewise should be anticipated with accuracy so that guesswork is eliminated, the mechanical details of makeup facilitated and costly revisions obviated. If the layout man is in doubt about composition specifications, he should consult the typographer who is to interpret the layout. In all cases the width and height of the text and cut areas and other display units should be marked in "picas"—a language the printer understands.

While looseness should be avoided and the typographical details specified with care, a layout should never be so "tight" as to require typographic makeup to a mathematical degree. A skillful typographer will always grasp the significance of whatever flexibility has been allowed in a layout and utilize it advantageously. A layout that is structurally sound will not deviate materially from the basic design pattern by standardization of spacing, margins and introduction of other typographical subtleties.

The Story of
The Quick Brown Fox
in the Composing Room

3. The compositor sets the foundry type to match the layout.

1. From experimental thumbnails, the design for a small booklet cover is chosen. An actual size layout is made and it goes to the composing room.

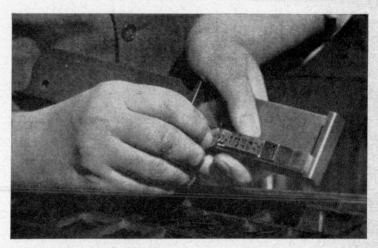

4. Deft hands skillfully space out a line of type with low, non-printing spaces and quads.

2. Type sizes are distinctly specified on the layout.

5. The setting completed, it is spaced horizontally to fit the layout.

6. The form is tied up and placed on the proof press.

Lengthy manuscript for text matter is set on the linotype, or perhaps on a monotype keyboard.

7. The first proof matches the layout. Composing room time and effort are saved by proper planning.

The ultimate objective of typographical layout. Skilled fingers of a compositor setting type with a layout made with preciseness and practicability.

The Ludlow also casts slugs of display type.

Ideas worth while are worthy
of worthwhile layout